What Leaders Are Saying About Leading
From The Power of a Clear Mind

"The world-wide economic crisis catapulted us into strategic changes that could have exploded into organizational chaos. Fortunately, our understanding of a clear leadership state of mind has kept us on track with innovative, creative action we never imagined possible. The roads are still difficult, but we have the right psychological gear."
~ VP, Heavy Equipment Manufacturing

"When I grasped the power and impact of my own state of mind, I realized my leadership responsibility was to create and tend to the culture of the organization. It shattered the walls of silos and set people free to experiment, learn, and create. I've never had more fun."
~ CEO, High Tech Industry

"Understanding the Power of a Clear Mind as a leadership principle changed my life, our team and our organization's life, and unleashed a torrent of creativity that allowed us to proactively respond to business crises in a way that surprised even Wall Street."
~ VP, Truck Engine Manufacturing

"Understanding the power of my own clear mind was a life altering personal and professional experience. In a new country with a different culture, my team also resonated with this principle. Collectively we harnessed that power and surpassed expectations of what was thought possible to do in a turn-around. We are tremendously grateful!"
~ Managing Director, Power Generation, Ghana

"When I finally understood that my own thinking—my distracted state of mind—was making me miserable and seeing a crisis around every corner, it was like a block of concrete being lifted from my shoulders. This understanding is liberating. I see options instead of barriers. I see colleagues instead of enemies. I feel present for whatever life places in front of me. And I know that my clarity of wisdom will help me find a way."

~ VP, Product Development,
Global Industrial Machinery

"This is a view on leadership unlike any I've ever heard. It fundamentally changed the way I lead and the way I live."

~ CFO, Health Care Industry

"The beauty of understanding the principles of leading from a clear state of mind is that it is life changing. No matter what event arises in any part of professional or personal life, I know that when my mind is clear I respond more creatively, proactively, and wisely. Individuals, teams, and organizations are more innovative and productive. Customers feel like partners. Family feels respected. It's easier to navigate the tides."

~ Managing Director, Global Engine
Manufacturing/Distribution, South Africa

"This isn't a series of steps and behaviors to memorize. It's an understanding—a realization that affects every part of life. I feel smarter, wiser, more productive, and more connected to people and possibility."

~ CEO, Telecommunications Industry

"Leading with a clear mind is powerful, profound, practical, and productive."

~ CEO, Biomedical Industry

"Our Senior Team had an awakening about our leadership responsibility beyond our organization. It expanded to our collective responsibility to the community. We began creating alliances and partnerships with institutions we previously viewed as competitors. Our new clarity helped us drop narrow ego-based decisions to focus on the real purpose of our mission."

~ COO, Health Care Industry

"I find the awareness of my state of mind to be one of the easiest and most powerful benefits of this understanding. I'm still in the traffic of life, but I'm more flexible. I can maneuver more easily. My awareness tells me if I'm in the right lane."

~ CEO, Insurance Industry

"On our continuing journey of increased clarity, we still work hard but with fewer struggles. We come to better decisions faster. There is higher quality output with less rework. People are more respectful, innovative, and curious. They want to learn about more than their own areas. They have a new relationship with internal and external customers. It's engaging, exhilarating, productive, and much simpler than before."

~ EVP, Banking Industry

"Our team is more productive, energetic, and creative than we've ever been with less wear and tear."

~ EVP, Technology Industry

"This understanding of leadership wiped away the cobwebs of command. My job is to unleash the genius in the organization, develop leaders, and create a culture of vibrant purpose. And, above all—to keep learning!"

~ EVP, Health Care Industry

Power of a Clear Mind

Power of a Clear Mind

The Direct Link Between
Your Leadership State of Mind
The Decisions You Make
The Actions You Take
The Results You Get

Penny Rock

Penny Rock • Woodside, California

Power of a Clear Mind

By Penny Rock

Other works by Penny Rock:

CDs
Power of a Clear Mind: Keep Your Bearings in Any Circumstance
The 8 Essential Ingredients of Healing: From Anything, Anywhere,
    Anytime
Available at www.powerofaclearmind.com

Books
He Called Me Lieutenant Angel: A Love Song From War
We Declare: The Truth About War and our Responsibility for Peace
Available at www.powerofaclearmind.com

Published by:
Penny Rock
www.powerofaclearmind.com

ISBN 978-0-9787156-4-9

First Printing 2011

Printed in the United States of America

Cover Design by JD Buckwell
Author Photo by Terry Gardner

Dedication

*For all who are dedicated to living and leading aligned
and integrated personal and professional lives that are:*

> *Inspired by a sense of purpose, meaning,
> fulfillment, and service*

> *Fueled by discovery, curiosity, exploration, insight,
> learning, change, and mastery*

> *Sustained by relationship, engagement,
> collaboration, interconnectedness, and mutual
> benefit*

Contents

PART ONE:
Profound Implications of a Clear Mind

A Principle-Based Foundation — Section 3

Leadership from the Power of a Clear Mind — Section 4

PART TWO:
Elements of a Clear Mind

The Power of a Clear Mind— The Source — Section 5

The Power of a Clear Mind— The Experience

Section 6

The Power of Listening— The Results

Section 7

PART THREE:
Practical Application and Evidence of a Clear Mind

Practical Integration   Section 10

Acknowledgments

The thoughts and understanding expressed in this book are, and will continue to be, a product of change, evolution, and new insight—never static. I have numerous thought partners from near and far who travel the road of discovery with me. They nudge or shove me into corners and crevices of understanding that could easily have eluded me without their presence on my own path of growth, learning, and living.

I will be forever grateful to Sydney Banks for sharing his understanding of the Principles of Mind, Consciousness, and Thought and for the impact that understanding continues to have on my life. I am also grateful for the opportunity to learn from and have deepening dialogue with teachers and friends such as Roger Mills, George Pransky, Keith Blevins, and Paul Nakai.

Special thanks to Tracey Carruthers, Robert Garner, and Joyce Leonard for their roles in bringing this book to life, and to my editor Marcia Ellett for her continued interest, patience, and encouragement.

PART ONE

Profound Implications of a Clear Mind

SECTION ONE

Introduction

CHAPTER ONE

Purpose of the Book

This book is the primary reference source for participants in Power of a Clear Mind (PCM) Executive Leadership Development sessions. It is meant to stimulate dialogue about a topic rather than serve as a comprehensive treatise on any one subject.

Consistent with the foundation of Power of a Clear Mind Leadership, the book is not a series of steps and techniques to be practiced. It consists of articles designed to elicit reflective thinking about how these topics present themselves in the lives of the participants.

All materials are insight-based. They are designed to stimulate insights from innate wisdom and are therefore meant to be read, viewed, and listened to repeatedly for increased learning and discovery. Audio and visual products are provided as companion pieces to written materials to deepen and broaden the foundational understanding of specific topics.

Preview of the Session

The interactive teaching method includes topic presentation, individual reflection, partner or group dialogue, and sharing of practical examples and insights. The teaching methodology creates a learning environment in which participants will be in a more receptive state of mind to understand their own innate capacities and thinking patterns. When patterns of thinking are understood, participants see the direct relationship between the quality of their thinking and their actions and results.

All sessions focus on deepening the understanding of the foundation of the Power of a Clear Mind at the individual level. As personal understanding increases, implications for interpersonal relationships and organizational impact are explored.

Because the capacity for a clear mind is *inside* everyone, and not contingent on anything *external*, this foundational understanding permeates all aspects of our lives—business, family, and community—enhancing the quality of life in *all* arenas.

CHAPTER TWO

Reflective Questions

Part of the Power of a Clear Mind teaching methodology is reflection on each topic discussed to determine personal and professional relevance and to deepen understanding.

Here are some sample questions to help you discover your own insights about any topic and its personal and professional impact.

- What does this topic mean to you? How is it relevant in your life?

- What is an example of how you have noticed this topic in your life?

- Why is it important and useful to know about this topic? Why are you grateful to know about it?

CHAPTER THREE

Glossary of Terms

Clear/Open Mind:

A clear/open mind is not an *empty* mind. Thoughts continually parade through our minds. A clear/open mind is not attached to any single thought, but is in a state of *readiness to receive* thoughts in the form of ideas and insights which will organize themselves into something useful.

Leading/Consulting/Coaching:

PCM Consulting helps leaders, consultants, and coaches discover and have faith in their own natural wisdom. The philosophy is relevant regardless of role.

In each role, a partnership with others is created for the purpose of discovery and development of innate capacities to be more aware and responsive in dealing with personal, interpersonal, and organizational situations, events and conditions.

The method is reflective, conversational, and exploratory in tone. The focus for decision making is one of *increasing* Mental Clarity and *decreasing* Mental Distraction.

Innate Human Capacities:

The mind's default setting for a clear/open mind. These *internal capacities* allow us to be responsive to *all external conditions* without Mental Distraction.

Listening for Clarity:

Listening without pre-conceived notions or opinions to hear and understand someone's spoken and unspoken message.

Reflective Thinking:

Reflective thinking is *not* a reflective or meditative *process*. It is the *quality* of thinking in a clear/open mind which is restful, receptive, and not cluttered with mental distractions. It is not contingent on time or procedures and therefore is available at all times *regardless* of quiet or urgent conditions.

State of Mind:

State of mind is simply the quality of our thinking at any given moment.

CHAPTER FOUR

Permissions and Disclosures

Use of Power of a Clear Mind™ (PCM) Materials, Processes, Products, and Methodology

Don't Even THINK of Doing This:

Use substantially exact copies of PCM work claiming it is your authorship or ownership and/or without attribution to or gaining permission from PCM. All PCM work is protected under appropriate copyright and registration laws. Not only is it illegal, it would dismay and disappoint me. And besides, it's just not polite.

I ENCOURAGE You to Do This:

- If you love what you have read, seen, or heard in one of my courses and wish to share it with others, please do so with full attribution to PCM.

- If you would like to share some of this material with a group and feel you cannot yet put it into your own words, please share it with attribution.

- If you have created articles, procedures, or other materials based upon the PCM methodology and they are not substantial duplicates of my work, feel free to use them with others and give attribution to anything that is specifically the property of PCM.

- If you have created a training program or your own materials based upon, but not a substantial duplication of, PCM methodology, be sure to copyright them for your own protection.

- If you have created any material as a result of a greater understanding of the PCM methodology, please send me a copy. I love seeing the practical applications of participants in our courses. Let me know if you would be willing to let other participants see your work as samples to guide them in their approach.

- If you are interested in teaching the PCM methodology, please contact me.

- You may "reprint" first-level foundation articles printed herein online, as long as they remain complete and unaltered including the "about the author" information, and providing you send a copy of the "reprint" to penny@powerofaclearmind.com.

- Any other usage of first-level foundation articles printed herein is protected under copyright laws ©2011 Penny Rock. All rights reserved.

- For more information contact Penny at penny@powerofaclearmind.com.

Discover the Power of Your Own Clear Mind

As you can see, I am not in the business of withholding my understanding. Why? Because you already have the innate capacity of a clear mind which is your natural wisdom. I do not own your wisdom so how could I withhold it?

I am committed to helping people *discover their own innate ability* to live in a wise and clear state of mind.

I want you to use my materials, ideas, and methodology to enhance and deepen your own understanding. It will also benefit others with whom you come in contact in your personal or professional life. You will have the privilege of serving yourself and others by enjoying and learning from all that life has to offer.

A New Leadership Model

CHAPTER ONE

Evolution of Leadership in Business: Models to Achieve Results

B usiness has always been on a quest to find the optimum way to achieve results. The search has been a source of dilemma for every leader since time began. The problem? Results seem to require the efforts of human beings.

When tools and machines are invented, results are faster and at times more predictable. However, they still require the presence of people to create and use them. And, people are *not* predictable.

They become fatigued, injured, need to eat and sleep; they have families that apparently need some attention; some want to "specialize" in only one kind of task; and they even want to be compensated for their efforts.

Business, whether primitive or sophisticated, relies on the collective efforts of a variety of people with a variety of skills and talents, and a variety of behaviors. What do people in a business complain about the most? Here's a clue: it isn't skills and talents. The number one complaint in any business is the behavior of others. As self awareness increases, people even begin to complain about their *own* behaviors.

Unfortunately, when people venture out from the confines of business and go back to their homes and communities, things don't change. Families and friends have the same major complaint. They may identify *different* behaviors than a coworker, but it still boils down to behavior. Why doesn't the behavior change when the venue does?

Business and Psychology Converge

Why people do what they do and how to get them to change was not only the focus of early business models, it was also the focus of psychological models. If you chart the evolution of psychology, you will find its influence on business and education, and it continues to lead the way on the path of understanding the human being.

The convergence of psychology and business is apparent in the focus of industrial psychologists, specialties in organizational behavior and development, and a plethora of consultants, books, seminars, and training in how to deal with, cope with, and influence behavioral change in others and ourselves.

Primary Evolutionary Models

Each model has been helpful and instrumental in looking for what is best in people. The underlying assumption has been that there is a way for people to be productive, be at ease with others, and experience personal well-being.

Most leadership models focus on behaviors. PCM leadership focuses on the state of mind, the quality of thinking, which produces the behavior.

The three earlier models focus on an external source of productivity, ease, and well-being. Understanding and manipulating actions and behaviors is required.

The fourth model focuses on an internal source of productivity, ease, and well-being. Understanding state of mind, the quality of thinking that *produces* action and behavior, is discovered and developed.

Evolution of Leadership in Business

MODEL	ATTENTION	FOCUS	PURPOSE
Structure Based	Symptoms	Organizational Structure, Tasks, Systems, Policy Procedure	Breadth of Control
Behavior Based	Symptoms	Behaviors	Breadth of Influence
Concept Based	Symptoms	Behavior, Values, Concepts	Breadth of Ideas
Principle Based	Cure	State of Mind	Depth of Foundational Understanding

Characteristics and Assumptions of Each Model

Structure Based:

- Change occurs as a result of organizing differently and creating new policies and procedures.

- New policies and procedures are spelled out in increasing detail and specificity. New tasks, structures, and systems are created to monitor, measure, and enforce those policies.

- Compliance with changes is expected without question or comment.

- Much of this model is derived from the military where it worked very well to quickly mobilize large groups toward a specific goal. Hierarchy, chain of command, and control are basic features.

- The working assumption is that many people need to be told what to do and how to do it to ensure productivity and quality.

Behavior Based:

- Early behavioral research indicates that people perform better if they feel good about their jobs. They will be excited about their jobs if they feel valued and involved.

- Organizational and procedural changes are still made, but for the purpose of changing workforce behavior rather than only focusing on consistency.

- Compliance is still expected, but people are asked for input so they will feel included in the decision.

- There is a belief that people are motivated by external sources such as money, environment, and recognition. If their needs are met, they will be happy and do a good job.

- It is also believed that each person is motivated by something different, so broad *and* specific motivators must be identified to best influence the workforce.

- The working assumption is that external influence and motivation will increase a sense of satisfaction with the job, and therefore performance will improve.

Concept Based:

- It is believed to be a good idea for organizations to identify corporate values and corresponding behaviors so people will know what is expected of them.

- It is wise to consider that people may have their own set of personal values. People will change their behaviors if they see compatibility between their personal values and those of the business.

- Some people may not have good values, but it is possible to teach values.

- When people have discussions or shared experiences in a healthy environment, they will automatically behave in a new way.

- Due to a tendency to revert to previous behavior, the new behavior will only have a moderate to short shelf-life unless there are regular reinforcement mechanisms in place.

- The working assumption is that people are motivated by different things, most motivation is external, and internal motivation is also possible. Regardless of the source, mechanisms must be employed to create and reinforce new behavior.

Principle Based:

- It is our innate wisdom, our clear mind, which allows us to live in a value-based way. All people have the same amount of wisdom available. The difference in behavior depends on our level of understanding of the role of state of mind in creating our reality.

- The source of our experience, our personal reality, is thought, making all motivation internal.

- Values are internally discovered rather than externally installed.

- Our innate capacity for perspective tells us when to reorganize, create new strategy or structure, and how to involve people in a useful, credible, productive, and respectful way. People treated in a respectful way know they are valued.

- The working assumption is that the state of mind we are in is the engine that drives and determines the quality of our ideas, concepts, behaviors, and decisions.

CHAPTER TWO

What's Different About this Approach?

Many books have been written about leadership. Earlier books tended to be about the need to "motivate" people to do what you want them to do complete with examples of reward systems to maintain their loyalty and effort. Today's books tend to be more about how to "inspire" an organization and to lead with a compelling vision of success. They recommend clearing the mind of external concerns. However, these books are also usually filled with steps, techniques, theories, and concepts about "how to" lead from inspiration.

The question is, where does inspiration come *from*? What is the *source* of vision, inspiration, theories, and concepts? Is it something you get from others? Are some people just special? Or, could it be that everyone has the capacity for clear-minded inspiration within them?

I do not teach steps, mechanics, or techniques. My approach works no matter what your business is. There is no possible circumstance or business that could not benefit from the Power of a Clear Mind. The approach is different because I share my philosophical foundation with you and the underlying principles from which it is derived. I believe a clear mind and the natural wisdom it provides is inherent in each person. I want you to discover the power and simplicity of your own clear mind.

My philosophical foundation provides an understanding of the power and momentum of a clear mind and how that helps you to be more creative and decisive about *any* action you take. It removes the "burden" and "hard work" of leadership. Instead, your diligence is rewarded with greater responsiveness, fluidity, wisdom, and common sense.

This foundation permeates not only what I do, but also the way I do it. My clients and other consultants tell me this philosophy is life changing; they see relevance for business strategies, policies, employee relations, systems, family, and community involvement. They also say they have created a new relationship with themselves. That's right—themselves.

You will not need to sort through specific client scenarios to find relevance to your own circumstances. Reflective thinking is the only way to increase understanding. As you reflect on the topics presented, you may see practical examples relevant to your own current or future leadership problems, questions, and aspirations. I encourage you to consider your own examples through the lens of the Power of a Clear Mind philosophy. It's really up to you. I don't know if you will. I *do* know that you can.

CHAPTER THREE

Why Focus on Senior Leadership?

I specialize in working with senior leaders because of the scope of leverage and the level of impact. There is *nothing* senior leaders can do in an organization that does not have a full-scale impact. My preference is to work with senior leaders who are visionary, insatiably curious, eternal students, and open-minded enough to see themselves on the brink of transition and transformation. That's when they have an appetite to explore the realm of possibility in strong and courageous ways. Those are the people who understand that the future is not a rehash of past practice, but exists in the unknown—and they are unafraid to explore that arena.

In my earlier years, I was a turnaround artist. I'd go into organizations that were performing poorly—it might be seen in financial, legal, or product or service quality terms—but there was always a cultural component at the source of their difficulties. My role was to address those issues and set standards necessary to bring them back on track and take them beyond current status quo. Then I would search for and hire new senior leaders to take over and run the organization in a healthier way. And I would go somewhere else and repeat the process.

I worked with public and private businesses, elected officials, legal, human service organizations, forensic science—a real variety.

After eighteen years, I joined an international leadership consulting group. I was a Vice President, Senior. Engagement Leader and Executive Consultant and Coach. I worked with Fortune 500 executives—nationally and internationally—in fields such as telecommunications, banking, pharmaceutical research, manufacturing, high tech—even an internationally renowned orchestra company. I was with them for 16 years.

What I was *good at* was keeping my bearings in the midst of turmoil, and helping others find theirs. I could see genius, potential, and possibility where others could not. I would be sent to senior teams who were on the brink of transition or transformation—and to some on the brink of disaster—at least in their view.

These companies were used to having consultants and coaches, but their prior experience was primarily behavioral in nature.

I don't do that. I specialize in, and focus on, helping leaders discover and have faith in their innate capacity to have a clear mind. I do that by bringing to light the quality of thinking—the state of mind—that *produces* the behavior. Behavior isn't ignored, but it's only interesting in the context that it is the *product* of thought. It's not a beast to be tamed, merely understood. It becomes clear that focusing on the behavior is like closing the proverbial barn door after the horse is gone. It's a step too late.

My purpose was to help the senior teams grasp the fact that their circumstances (economy, technology, legislation, etc.) are *never* the source of their difficulties and dilemmas. No, the source of their pain and mental myopia is the quality of their thinking *about* those circumstances.

If they are short sighted, they can't see a way out.

If they can't see a way out—there won't be one. If they can't see possibility it's because their thinking is lost in the fog of fear.

And, fear is a very poor advisor.

Now these were smart people. They didn't get where they were because they were lightweights. And, usually they saw the direct link between thinking and behavior. Their big question was, "How can I tell what state of mind I'm in?"

The answer is not only simple, it's intuitive. And it's a relief once its power becomes clear. Our thinking produces feelings. Therefore, our feelings are the barometer of the quality of our thinking—our state of mind.

And everyone understands and has experienced that. When you are frustrated and stressed out, your decisions are more reactive and aren't as creative or effective. The feelings of frustration or stress are the signal your state of mind is not as clear.

When you are feeling calm, focused, optimistic, hopeful, even in the face of difficult odds, you're wise, decisive, proactive, responsive, and creative. Those feelings are the signal your state of mind is clearer.

When the stakes are highest, you want the clearest minds to prevail.

"What was I thinking?" becomes *"How* was I thinking?" Your feelings are like road signs; they tell you when it is safe to proceed.

Everyone has examples of that in their personal and professional lives. Each person reading this recognizes it.

Is there *any* circumstance in which you would *prefer not* to have a clear mind?

Why is it Essential for Senior Leaders to Understand the Source and Power of their Clear Mind—Especially Now When the Economy is Tight and Uncertain?

When the stakes are highest, you want the clearest minds to prevail.

Every leadership decision has an effect from the boiler room to the boardroom and beyond—all the way to the shareholders. When we're distracted by worry, fear, a self-image that is inflated or deflated, we play it safe, we acquiesce, we compete against each other. Decisions are either too slow to be effective or so reactionary they aren't relevant—or worse—they're destructive.

The power of a clear mind is not about sitting on a stump going into a trance. A clear mind is vibrant, vital, active, discerning, decisive, constructive, and inclusive. Creative juices flow with the strength and power of a waterfall.

Bottom-Line Benefits

The Power of a Clear Mind creates cultural and financial turnarounds.

When leaders don't pay attention to the collective organizational state of mind, decisions are often reactionary—fear based. There is a negative impact on the quality of performance and productivity at *every* level. Everything suffers—from financial stability, to management, workforce, and union relationships, to Wall Street reputations.

The deleterious effects also extend to the family. Leaders and members of the workforce are always talking about strained relationships at home and feeling pulled between organizational effectiveness and personal balance.

When leaders *do* pay attention to creating a clear-minded organizational state of mind, people stop in-fighting, silos disappear, and they are more creative, innovative, responsive, wise, and decisive. There is greater alignment to corporate vision, strategy, and goals that essentially eliminates time-wasting arguments and lip service. Decision-making and problem solving are streamlined, accelerated, and sacred cows become a thing of the past.

The Power of a Clear Mind strengthens the organizational immune system to create stability regardless of shifting priorities or economic, technological, and political turbulence. A clear-minded organization is more flexible and nimble so there is greater readiness for an economic turnaround.

Leading from a clear mind doesn't mean you're exempt from problems. But you can navigate them with greater wisdom and less physical and psychological wear and tear.

Problems are just problems. Events are just events. How well we deal with them is determined by our state of mind. And a clear state of mind is better than a distracted one.

The Leadership Imperative

The CEO has the responsibility to:

Set the vision:	The *Why* and the *What* of the business.
Determine overall strategy:	*How* business vision will be approached and attained.
Create cultural standards:	The *Way* in which business is conducted internally and externally.

The Shift Begins and Sustains When Senior Leaders

- **Understand** their role and responsibility to set the organizational standard to recognize, develop, and unleash leadership talent at all levels.

- **Inspire** the creation of an organizational culture infused with profound thinking, practical solutions, and the proactive search for possibility.

- **Strengthen** the organizational immune system to create stability regardless of shifting priorities or economic, technological, and political turbulence.

- **Discern** the difference between clear wisdom and strong opinion.

- **Recognize** the genius and wisdom in others.

Two Secret Ingredients for Leadership Success

In the landmark research that resulted in the book *Good to Great*, the authors and researchers found that consistently high performing CEOs possessed two key qualities: humility and resolve. These ingredients seemed to put some CEOs in front of the industry pack. The researchers were not able to explain how these qualities came about, but they were consistent.

Here is my view of the key elements of those qualities as they relate to the Power of a Clear Mind.

Humility

- Open mind
- Insatiable curiosity and desire to learn
- Committed to continuous development of self and organization

The researchers expected to find more arrogance than humility. Arrogance is actually a weak position from which to lead because it drowns out the voice of natural wisdom. It is all about personal ego, which closes the mind and eliminates the possibility of learning.

Resolve

- Having a clear mind is a *priority* for decision-making.
- Unafraid to take risks.
- Unafraid to make unpopular decisions.

When humility and resolve are present in senior leadership, increased mutual respect and credibility are instilled between leadership, employees, customers, boards, shareholders, and Wall Street.

What is the "POWER" of a Clear Mind and Why is it Life Changing?

One-Stop Shopping

The *simplicity and ease* of making decisions as a result of understanding the Power of a Clear Mind is that there is only one place to look when you embark on *any* kind of decision-making. It will help you if you are hiring or firing, starting a business, dropping a product line, restructuring a business, or entering into a new relationship. *Anything.*

The *power* is that a clear mind is an innate capacity. And because it is innate, your mental well-being is secure; it's not in the hands of other people or outside circumstance. You can count on its presence.

When you discover how to know when your mind is clear, and how to have faith in and depend on its presence regardless of the circumstance, the Power of a Clear Mind is not just business changing, it's life changing!

A Principle-Based Foundation

CHAPTER ONE

Why Foundation First?

It may seem obvious why it is helpful to understand foundation first. However, in the realm of leadership there is often a desire to "get right to the specifics." People want steps and templates.

It's easy to understand why, but in the field of human functioning, it would be detrimental to put the cart before the horse. So, let's take a look at the basics.

Foundation Determines the Strength, Flexibility, and Application of Whatever Comes Next.

When doctors study the body, they must first understand basic anatomy and the function of individual systems and their interdependence as a whole. Once the physical foundation is understood, specialties become beneficial.

We operate on a philosophical foundation continuum that provides us with a navigation system for how we live our lives. We look to our foundation for the standards we set for how we live in a global society. It determines our decisions on a spectrum from generosity to greed, tolerance to judgment, contribution to destruction, and service to entitlement. It is the voice of what we call our conscience.

Businesses also have a philosophical foundation. Whether or not it is articulated, it is made apparent by the decisions made and the relationships with employees, customers, the community, boards, shareholders, and Wall Street. Leaders need to understand their own philosophical foundation and how it determines what they do and how and why they do it. It is important for them to understand the role of their state of mind, not only in how their philosophical foundation is derived, but in how it expresses itself and impacts their results.

The clearer we are about our philosophical foundation the more congruent are our actions and behaviors with our standards, and the more we keep our bearings in any circumstance. If we had no philosophical foundation, our sense of well-being would be at the whim of external forces.

Reflective Questions

What resonates with you in this chapter?

What surprises you about this chapter?

What are you curious to learn more about?

Bonus Question

When have you noticed a philosophical foundation operational in a business? In what way(s)?

My Insights

CHAPTER TWO

Foundation Principles

The Purpose of Principles

Principles give us something in which to have faith. We count on them to hold true and function the same way at all times, removing the element of chance, luck, or fluke. They are defined as providing a basic truth or source.

The Nature of Principles

Principles exist *before* their properties can be understood, described, or explained. They are discovered and realized rather than created.

Principles are universal in application and in action at all times, for all people, throughout the world, in all circumstances—much like gravity. Most of us don't worry about losing our grip on the planet. We may not be able to explain it very well, can't touch it or taste it, but we have faith that gravity isn't capricious and we're not in danger of flying off into space with our next step. We don't have to "gain access" to it because it's just there. We have faith in its existence and constancy.

Principles are neutral. They act the same way for everyone. They do not place judgments on good, bad, pleasant, unpleasant, right or wrong.

Principles provide simplicity within complexity and are the same over time. Gravity works the same for us as it did for our ancestors, and will be the same for future generations.

The Search to Describe the Human Experience

Through the ages, philosophers, scientists, those in the healing arts, and others have tried to explain the nature of the human experience. Many constructs point to the external environment as the impetus for our thoughts, feelings, and actions. Wisdom is either learned or earned, or the purview of the few. We are products of our environment and circumstances, and only the very brave can rise above their legacy.

Such constructs are concepts, ideas, and models, but they do not meet the criteria of principles. The search for a way to describe the human experience is admirable and has been valuable and beneficial. Many models have provided a platform for further exploration and insight. However, even more modern and evolving models still leave us as ink on the pen of an external writer rather than the authors of our lives.

The following principles were articulated by the philosopher and author Sydney Banks. Contrary to prevailing cultural views, we are not controlled by the puppet strings of circumstance. The understanding of these principles is that each human being has the innate capacity to experience life from the inside out.

Three Principles of Human Experience

- **Mind** – A universal energy and intelligence in all things.

- **Thought** – Our ability to create ideas, images, and concepts.

- **Consciousness** – The ability to experience our thoughts as "reality", through our feelings/senses—our state of mind, and to know we are the thinker.

Mind is the energy that governs our ability to create mental images that create our experience of life through the power of Thought. Consciousness allows us to be aware of the fact that we are the thinker, and to be aware of the experience that we have created for ourselves.

For example, two people have a change in their working environment. One person sees opportunity in the change; the other sees disruption in their familiar routine. A circumstance has changed, and these two people experienced that change differently via their respective thoughts *about* the circumstance. The Three Principles in practical action.

NOTE: In this context, Mind does not refer to the brain. The brain is the vehicle or conduit through which thoughts and consciousness are processed and experienced. Similarly, the electric outlet and cord are not the source of electricity. They serve only as the vehicle or conduit for the transmission of its energy.

Bottom Line

We have innate health and resilience regardless of the circumstances we face. Our well-being is not contingent upon external influences. We are our own thinker. *We* create our individual "reality" through our thoughts, and experience the reality we have created through our feelings—our state of mind.

When we realize we are the authors of our lives, there is a tremendous sense of relief and hope that we can live more enjoyable and productive personal and professional lives.

Reflective Questions

What resonates with you in this chapter?

What surprises you about this chapter?

What are you curious to learn more about?

Bonus Question

What is an example of how you have noticed the Three Principles of Mind, Consciousness, and Thought in your life?

My Insights

CHAPTER THREE

Principles in Practice

Personal and Professional

The three Principles of Human Experience are expressed in our daily lives in ways both practical and profound. Mind allows us to see ourselves and others as part of something bigger in life than our individual separate existence. We have a sense of purpose and meaning. Consciousness allows us to experience and learn from our insights. We see the possibility and necessity of learning and discovery. Thought allows us to be autonomous, examine gaps in our integrity, and create beneficial relationships. We see the power, efficiency, and joy of creating and engaging in collective relationships.

Simply stated, the Principles of Human Experience can be expressed in our daily lives as personal and professional principles of Purpose and Meaning, Learning and Discovery, and Relationship and Connection.

Purpose & Meaning

I would be hard put to find a person or a business that did not have a sense of purpose and meaning. They may not articulate it in those terms, but when asked questions about when they feel fulfilled, what they find inspiring, or what ignites their passion, they are not at a loss for words.

When asked, people talk about giving back, being of service, helping others, reaching out, teaching, mentoring, developing others, creating, having a sense of mission, vision, values, and fulfillment. In business, part of creating value and serving a vision includes invention, innovation, production, and profit. Purpose and meaning always include the profound and the practical.

They also speak of feeling guided or directed by a gentle yet substantial force. They speak of a beacon that sheds light on the path to follow. The words are expansive yet they convey simplicity.

Purpose and Meaning are not words—they are a feeling within a state of mind. And the state of mind in which they are conceived and experienced will determine their profundity, expansiveness, and impact.

Individuals rely on a sense of purpose and meaning to make practical decisions about how they live their lives at home and in the community.

Businesses rely on a sense of purpose and meaning to provide a compass for strategy, goals, and the organizational culture in which they are achieved.

Learning & Discovery

Have you ever met a child who didn't love to learn? Who wasn't curious? Who didn't want to explore?

All people have an innate desire and capacity to learn, discover, have insights, create, innovate, master a practice, learn in depth and breadth, make connections between one learning and another, improvise, experiment, and to change.

A learning life is vibrant, fulfilling, and humble. There is an insatiable curiosity and desire to explore the unknown, and a profound respect for the capacity to learn and the effort and commitment it requires. This is true throughout life—child and adult—personal and professional.

Organizations also have lives. Those that stifle learning become fearful, insular, and arrogant. They become the poster for the "not invented here" mentality. They become stagnant.

Organizations that value learning see no boundaries in knowledge. They actively look for opportunities to learn, grow, and expand their consciousness. They have the courage to find out what they don't know and look for the people who can teach them. Sources of learning are unrestricted. They include experts in related and unrelated fields, customers, and clients. They even value what people in other departments might have to teach them!

Purpose and Meaning are not words—they are a feeling within a state of mind. And the state of mind in which they are conceived and experienced will determine their profundity, expansiveness, and impact.

Individuals rely on the ability to learn and discover, the understanding of the value of patience and practice, the pragmatism to change and adapt, and the strength and agility to challenge perceived limits.

Businesses rely on the ability to learn and discover, create a culture that can challenge current assumptions and strategy, see obvious and hidden opportunities, harness energy to invent, blend technology, increase flexibility to change, and see the untapped reservoir of customers and their needs.

Relationship and Connection

Did you ever have an imaginary friend? I did. Her name was Amy. We played together, talked to each other, laughed together, wept together, and shared our dreams—even if it was as simple as wanting to walk to the corner without an adult holding our hands, or as grand as planning a visit to the moon. Most of the time, she lived in my home. But, sometimes, she went to faraway places. At those times we talked on the phone. She would visit friends on another block or new friends in India. Naturally we both spoke the language of wherever she was.

From our earliest moments in life, we form relationships. We make connections with people. One of the first relationships we explore is our relationship with ourselves. Just as Amy was a way for me to learn about and share and express more of myself.

The qualities we value in relationships emerge in our youth and we hold them dear forever. Qualities such as respect, listening without judgment, emotional security, empathy, autonomy and partnership, vitality and resilience, non-contingency, the ability to toss around ideas and dreams, generosity, and forgiveness to name a few. These qualities become the touchstone for every relationship in our lives, both personal and professional.

Organizations are made up of collective relationships. The quality of those relationships and the depth of connection experienced are the determining factors in the quality of the organizational culture. And those relationships are both internal and external. By default, a healthy culture creates healthy relationships

Principles are identified separately but understood and experienced collectively. They are an integrated whole.

with customers, clients, the community, and even competitors.

Relationships are the building blocks for colleagues, teams, divisions, and departments. People are naturally able to blend the needs of their group with those of the company.

Personal expression is expected within collaboration. It becomes common sense to engage the thinking of others to solve problems, design systems, assess the impact of decisions, systems, or technology across the organization, and commit to transparency throughout functions. People see, expect, and experience interconnection between parts of the organization. There is a visceral understanding that silos are for corn cobs.

Individuals rely on relationships and connection to create partnerships, experience engagement, and enlarge their experience of life, without sacrificing personal autonomy.

Businesses rely on relationships and connection to build trusted, supportive, expansive, dynamic, and efficient teams that operate with autonomy and integrity.

Bottom Line

It's in our nature as human beings to look for meaning in life, to explore higher ideals, to reach out to those who may need a hand, to be of service. It's in our nature to be curious, to want to learn, to practice, and to master. It's in our nature to be social, to find a sense of connection with others well beyond the structure of family.

The principles discussed above are a way of describing those aspects of our nature—and they are universal. They function the same way across time, geography, gender, and culture.

Principles are identified separately but understood and experienced collectively. They are an integrated whole. For example, math has four principles. Although we initially learn about addition, subtraction, multiplication, and division separately, we can't completely understand math until we understand how these principles operate together.

Once we understand the principles of purpose and meaning, learning and discovery, and relationship and connection, we can experience how they not only *can* operate together, but are required to do so. Only then do we see the implications and applications for how we live our lives. Only then can businesses understand that principles are foundational guides rather than slogans. When they do, businesses become vibrant, creative, resilient entities regardless of economic storms.

You could say that individuals and businesses are:

- Inspired by purpose and meaning
- Fueled by learning and discovery
- Sustained by relationship and connection

Not a bad way to live an aligned and integrated personal *and* professional life.

Reflective Questions

What resonates with you in this chapter?

What surprises you about this chapter?

What are you curious to learn more about?

Bonus Question

What is an example of how you have noticed the Three Principles of Purpose, Learning, and Relationship in your life?

My Insights

CHAPTER FOUR

The Unique Competitive Advantage

Principle-Based Leadership

The demand in organizations today is for a quality of leadership that is astute, resilient, trustworthy, and light-hearted, setting a cultural tone of healthy high performance. People want to deliver to performance expectations; they want to do their best and they want to feel good within their work environment, especially during times of organizational change.

Awareness of the importance of leadership development is long-standing. There are many courses and training organizations offering leadership development approaches. For the most part, these offerings are behavioral based and, although effective to a degree, approach development issues by addressing behavior directly. Change can occur as long as the techniques for imparting change are remembered and implemented. Consequently, change efforts often fade with time, and the organizational system can default to previous ineffective ways of operating.

A principle-based, insight-driven approach results in sustainable change over time. Change resulting from insight becomes long-term because the logic behind the change effort derives from a perceptual shift. With such a perceptual shift, people do not have to remember techniques to sustain change. Different and more practical ways of attaining goals occur to them from their own reflective thinking.

Organizational needs and circumstances are perceived as creative indicators for potential improvement. Insight on how to move forward transforms the fear of change into the inspiration of understanding how to achieve results. Change then appears as the next logical step to take to achieve desired goals, and it becomes not only sustainable but also effortless.

A principle-based, insight-driven approach results in sustainable change over time.

Understanding this principle-based leadership approach teaches people how to develop dependable, innate leadership attributes in an on-going evolutionary way, taking creative and pragmatic cues from their own wisdom and expertise. With principle-based leadership, integrity, accountability, trust, and creativity begin to permeate the organizational climate, as choices are made from an informed and reflective state of mind. Organizations and the people in them can then weather the demand for change as they embrace it from clarity and certainty.

In Summary:

Traditional Leadership Development	Principle-Based Leadership Development
Behavior driven	Insight driven
Short-term change impact: the system can default to previous less effective ways of operating	Sustainable change over time: the system continues to address evolving demands
Relies on techniques for effective change strategies	Perceptual shift allows for creative, effortless problem-solving
Coping strategies to address fear of change	Fear is transformed into inspiration and an understanding about how to achieve results
Change seen as hard work and effortful	Change seen as the logical next step to achieve desired results and is effortless

Reflective Questions

What resonates with you in this chapter?

What surprises you about this chapter?

What are you curious to learn more about?

Bonus Question

How would understanding Principle-Based Leadership be of benefit to the organization? The way you lead?

My Insights

Leadership from the Power of a Clear Mind

CHAPTER ONE

Purpose Centered and Service Oriented

Now that we have a better understanding of how we experience life, it's time to look deeper into how our three foundation principles and state of mind inform and inspire a business foundation, philosophy, and methodology.

The Leadership State of Mind

Leadership is not a position—it is a state of mind that stems from something bigger than ourselves. Whatever work we do is a manifestation of what we believe our purpose to be. Our purpose should be in alignment with who we are, and should serve our clients' needs. Being in service to our clients is about entering a partnership to help them realize and release their own potential.

The Leader's Clients

Who are the leader's clients? They are encompassed in a 360-degree arc. Clients include the senior leadership team, the employees in every role, unions, shareholders, private, public, and political governing boards, customers, the public, the community in which you live, the community and industry you serve, and Wall Street.

Sound daunting? It doesn't need to. When leadership is viewed through the narrow lens of balance sheets, legal requirements, and Wall Street deadlines it becomes confining and unfulfilling. No wonder there is such a high incidence of stress related physical, psychological, and relationship distress at the top of the ladder.

When leaders are operating from a purpose greater than the obvious details in a corporate mission statement, they actually accomplish more of what is required with less stress and effort. The privilege of serving the larger client base unleashes bottomless depths of creative potential and becomes a reservoir of possibility and a source of fulfillment.

> *Leadership is not a position—it is a state of mind that stems from something bigger than ourselves.*

Simplicity vs. Complexity

There is an elegant simplicity to this approach. It begins and ends with listening. What *we* make of our clients' situations is of little value. When we hear what *they* make of their situations, and more importantly, when *they* hear what they make of them, insights occur and that is of enormous value.

Leadership from a Clear Mind helps people access, and learn to have faith in, their innate wisdom. When they experience their *own* insights, *that's* when change occurs.

Reflective Questions

What resonates with you in this chapter?

What surprises you about this chapter?

What are you curious to learn more about?

Bonus Question

How would you describe your personal sense of purpose?

My Insights

CHAPTER TWO

A Leadership Approach

Different from the Norm

Leadership from the Power of a Clear Mind is a "wellness" versus an "illness" model. I don't look for what's wrong with a person or organization. I look for evidence of innate wisdom and untapped potential, and point that out to them. My model focuses on the *quality of thinking* that produces sustained systemic change.

Some conventional leadership models point to external conditions and repetitive behaviors as the source of focus and clarity. Those models concentrate on individual behavioral change. I believe this sets people looking in the wrong direction.

We all have situations, conditions, and events in our lives. How we navigate them is a function of the quality of our thinking—our state of mind.

We all know people who have been through a harrowing situation. Yet one person maintains equilibrium and learns from the experience, while another is tormented the rest of his life. Relying on our naturally clear, reflective, wise state of mind is the reason we can maintain equilibrium when the earth is moving beneath us.

The events of our lives are merely those—events. The way we think *about* those events is the difference between heaven and hell.

State of Mind – Practicality and Simplicity

When people understand that their state of mind is what produces their results, they have only one place to look for an answer to a dilemma—*the quality of their thinking.* They remain cognizant of unhealthy behaviors, but they have insights into the unhealthy thinking that produced them in the first place. Their natural wisdom allows them to make changes with less effort, because it *makes sense* to them to do so.

There is no need for a list of seventeen behaviors to practice, six mantras to spout, five books to read, three weeks of vacation, sixty laps around the track, or, well, you get the point. A person might indeed do any of these things, but only because it makes sense to *them*, not because they are someone else's prescription for peace.

> *We all have situations, conditions, and events in our lives. How we navigate them is a function of the quality of our thinking—our state of mind.*

People inherently understand that when they are thinking clearly, they get better results. They are more reflective, creative, and concise in decision making, problem solving, and conflict resolution; and resilient in what others perceive as crisis. They get more done, achieve better results in less time, feel less stress, and experience a better quality of life. They know this to be true. They just aren't certain of the source of this focused state of mind.

Reflective Thinking

Many people say it's easy to have a quiet state of mind when things are going well, but during stressful times, when things aren't going well, they just can't seem to find the ideal place or enough quiet time to think clearly. I do not recommend that you go searching for the highest mountain to sit on in your quest for enlightenment or a little levitation above the fray.

Having a clear, reflective, undistracted state of mind is not contingent on peaceful surroundings.

Reflective thinking is a state of mind. It is not a condition to be practiced or sought. It is not contingent on time, place, person, circumstance, age, or gender. It is an innate capacity. We can't avoid all difficult circumstances in life, nor should we try. One person's difficult circumstance is someone else's adventure. Life provides events. Our job is to navigate them as best we can and learn from the experience. A reflective state of mind allows us to operate at optimum capacity during the process.

Results Oriented

There is a bottom-line benefit to understanding that our state of mind governs our experience of life and our resilience to the circumstances we face. Even in times of turmoil our natural wisdom elicits a quiet and reflective state of mind, a requirement for making swift, smart decisions that may save a friendship, client relationship, departmental budget, a corporate reputation on Wall Street, or our lives.

Reflective Questions

What resonates with you in this chapter?

What surprises you about this chapter?

What are you curious to learn more about?

Bonus Question

When have you paid attention to your state of mind before making a decision?

My Insights

CHAPTER THREE

Philosophy

Form Follows Philosophy

What we do, why we do it, and the way we do it, stems from some underlying beliefs, values, and principles—a personal philosophy—we hold dear about the most effective way to get results. The actions we take are the "form" that follows that "philosophy." And, form *always* follows philosophy, never the other way around.

All leaders have a philosophy that provides a roadmap for how they conduct business, and how they deal with their various constituencies. They may not have written a statement of philosophy, but all of them can tell you about their beliefs and assumptions about their preferred way to get results. They may go on to tell you about how they have emulated other leaders.

Our personal philosophy—invisible though it may seem—is the foundation for the way in which we live our lives.

Philosophy is Straightforward

My philosophy is pretty simple. It begins and ends with understanding the power and role of a clear state of mind in our well-being. Our state of mind determines the quality and effectiveness of our thinking, actions, and results. All people have the same capacity for a clear mind and have innate psychological health available to them regardless of circumstance.

Would you like to:

- Generate more creative and profitable business solutions?

- Make all decisions with greater clarity, focus, and economy?

- Create an organization that is swift, nimble, flexible, and aligned?

- Solve personal and professional conflicts more easily?

- Create healthier personal and professional relationships?

- Discover how to have greater balance, meaning and fulfillment in *every* aspect of life?

If your answer is yes to any or all of these questions, I want you to know it is completely within your power to accomplish any of these goals. It's within the power of your clear state of mind. *Every* decision to be made or problem to be solved is more effectively done when your mind is clear.

Makes sense, doesn't it? When was the last time you preferred to have an unclear mind? When did you want less wisdom, common sense, or perspective? So, where can you *get* a clear mind?

Everything you need to live a healthy and productive professional and personal life is already inside you. My job is to help you discover and have faith in your own natural resources. And when you do, you are no longer at the mercy of external conditions or whim. You are able to see yourself with enough perspective to notice when you are going down a path of folly. You actually begin to consult with and coach yourself.

You also have the presence of mind to know how, when, and to whom you should look when you want a trusted advisor for additional perspective.

Each of us has innate capacities such as wisdom, insight, and perspective. These and other capacities are most powerful when fueled by a clear state of mind. It helps you keep your bearings *regardless of the circumstances* surrounding you.

Wouldn't you like to live a life of greater resilience without being buffeted around by the storms of circumstance? I'm *not* saying you will never experience difficult or painful situations. Those are part of the natural human experience. I *am* saying you can navigate those situations with greater clarity and equilibrium.

The role of state of mind in your life is simple, practical, and profound. It is the source of your discontent and delight, your questions and your answers, your confusion and your clarity. It is one-stop shopping. You need look no further for the answers to your dilemmas or the location of your peace.

Reflective Questions

What resonates with you in this chapter?

What surprises you about this chapter?

What are you curious to learn more about?

Bonus Question

How would you describe your own philosophical foundation?

My Insights

CHAPTER FOUR

Methodology

A Journey of Discovery

Whether I'm a leader of an organization, a consultant, or a coach, my methodology of working with people is the same. I share this methodology with you so you can consider its relevance to your role in any area of your professional or personal life.

My methodology is one of partnership on your journey of personal discovery. Personal discovery *always* precedes professional discovery because *who you are* governs *what you do*. You are the expert in your life or business. I am here to help you learn how to listen to your own wisdom and to discover the power of your own clear mind so your personal and professional life is more fulfilling and profitable.

Insights produce sustainable change in approach and behaviors because the quality of your thinking has changed.

A Safe and Painless Process

Because my philosophy is thought-based rather than behavior-based, you will learn about and experience your own clear state of mind. There is no need to go on an expedition searching for someone else's wisdom. You won't need to dredge up the past, memorize a list of dos and don'ts, or practice a series of behaviors. And you won't be judged.

Listening

I listen to you rather than the other way around. Prior to working with you, I will interview you to learn what's on your mind, why you want a consultant or coach, what your experience with either has been, why it's of value to you, and what your expectations are. Once we begin the process, I will listen for clarity not only about your circumstances, but more importantly, what you *make* of those circumstances. You will also learn to listen differently, not only to others but to yourself.

Dialogue

We will have dialogue about your questions and concerns, and identify areas in which you wish to expand and develop. You'll talk about your aspirations and what you find inspiring. Throughout our dialogue, we will explore your understanding of how your state of mind either expands or limits who you are and what you do.

Reflection

Reflection allows you to gaze at your thoughts. It is a state of mind, not a series of procedures or techniques. I'll ask you some questions that will help you explore your own thinking about relevant topics. You will be able to explore an idea from several angles because you will have the distance of perspective. The process of reflection allows you to observe, examine, and question your beliefs, opinions, and values in a nonjudgmental way. You can see how or if they are integrated into all aspects of your life. Reflection is a marvelous way to consider the views and wisdom of others to see what *you* make of them.

Insights

Insights can only occur in a clear mind, and they are a natural product of reflection. Thoughts will spring to mind that provide sudden clarity. They can be both practical and profound, and will be relevant and meaningful because they are *your* insights. Someone else's insights are interesting but only serve as thought-provoking ideas. You cannot have vicarious insights. Insights produce sustainable change in approach and behaviors because the quality of your thinking has changed.

Experience

Between our sessions, you will be applying what you have learned and discovered in areas of your life where it resonates most or seems most relevant at the moment. What you learn transcends what you are doing, where you are doing it, and with whom you are doing it. Your understanding is not contingent upon anything or anyone.

The process of leading, consulting, or coaching is not linear. We move among the areas listed above fluidly depending upon your need, curiosity, and topics relevant to you.

Likewise, as you begin to integrate this methodology into your life, you will increase your ability to listen deeply, engage in more relevant dialogue, explore your reflective thinking in a nonjudgmental state of mind, experience meaningful insights, and help others apply what they have learned to all aspects of their professional and personal lives.

Reflective Questions

What resonates with you in this chapter?

What surprises you about this chapter?

What are you curious to learn more about?

Bonus Question

How would understanding the Power of a Clear Mind philosophy and methodology help you as a leader?

My Insights

PART TWO

Elements of a Clear Mind

The Power of a Clear Mind— The Source

CHAPTER ONE

The Power of a Clear Mind

It Just Comes Naturally

Have you ever been in what others would call a hectic environment, but you were calm, responsive, and decisive? Have you ever been in what others would call a quiet environment, but you were in a mental snowstorm? We've all been in both situations. Have you ever wondered what accounted for your ability to navigate these circumstances in such different and seemingly counterintuitive ways?

The difference is that in the first scenario you were experiencing the power of a clear mind. In the second, you were experiencing the frustrations of a distracted mind. Okay, sounds reasonable. But, how do you *get* your mind to clear? Can you do it at will? Yes, but only if you don't *try*. How's that for counterintuitive?

To be able to clear your mind, you must understand what it is and is not.

Nothing can hold a clear mind hostage. There is nothing inherently bad or frightening unless we experience fearful thoughts. Our capacity for a clear mind allows us to handle difficult situations in any location at any time in a healthy, responsive manner.

Key Points—A Clear Mind is:

Free of Distraction:

Not physical distraction but mental distraction. Athletes engaged in vigorous activity frequently speak of being calm and responsive when to the observer it looks like chaos all around them. Their minds are not focused on the fans, other players, or the bruise on their leg. They are completely *present* in the moment and therefore responsive to the *needs* of the moment.

Non-Contingent:

There is no cause and effect relationship to time, location, or circumstance. Nor is a clear mind contingent upon whether we *like* our circumstances or the results of our decisions.

A Natural Open Channel:

In their natural state, our thought waves are static free, much as a radio is when tuned to a clear frequency. When we are mentally distracted and think circumstances are the cause of our lack of clarity, our thought waves become clogged and the channel's reception is compromised.

The Power of a Clear Mind is that it makes us open receptacles for valuable information to help us respond effectively. Without this capacity, we would be at the mercy of whim. A clear mind is nonselective and allows us to be present in *all* situations in our lives. A clear mind benefits our work, relationships, physical and mental health—our entire life.

There is no possible circumstance or event in our lives that does not benefit from a clear mind. Not one. That's its power *and* its beauty.

Three Principles of Human Experience

- **Mind**: A universal energy and intelligence in all things.
- **Thought**: Our ability to create images, ideas, and concepts.
- **Consciousness**: The ability to experience our thoughts as "reality", through our feelings/senses—our state of mind, and to know we are the thinker.

What is State of Mind?

State of Mind: The quality of our thinking at any point in time. Our state of mind fluctuates constantly on a continuum between clarity and distraction.

Help! How Do I Know What State of Mind I'm In?

A Clear Mind Is	A Clear Mind Is Not
Non-judgmental	Critical
Energetic; Vital	Bored; Pressured
Creative; Experimental	Passive; Procrastinating
Hopeful	Fearful; Judged; Judging
Present; In the moment	Worried; Angry; Resentful

Reflective Questions

What resonates with you in this chapter?

What surprises you about this chapter?

What are you curious to learn more about?

Bonus Question

How was the power of your clear mind beneficial to you in a difficult circumstance? Describe.

My Insights

CHAPTER TWO

The Thought Cycle

Round and Round It Goes

Have you ever found yourself in a quandary and said, "I need to get my thinking straight?" How did you know your thinking needed an adjustment? Was it something you felt? Was it worry, confusion, doubt, or maybe anxiety?

Have you ever found yourself straining to climb a steep hill or several flights of stairs? You may have said to yourself, "I need to use my knees more to lift my body, or maybe I need to get my body in better shape." How did you know your body needed adjustment? Was it something you felt in your knees or your back or your breathing?

Strange as it may seem, our bodies and minds work in similar fashion. If you feel knee discomfort, it makes sense to check the quality of your body's position or your state of health. If you feel mental discomfort, it makes sense to check the quality of your thinking or your state of mind.

Natural Wisdom

In both scenarios it naturally makes sense to us that the quality of our physical and mental health is the answer to our challenges.

It appears obvious that we are complicit in our body's discomfort. It may be less obvious that we are also complicit in our mental discomfort. Once we understand how the human thought process works, it becomes clear where to look for the point of adjustment when we feel mentally off-track.

The mental adjustment is not a forceful act. It's not a series of positive affirmations. It's far more subtle. Just understanding that the quality of thought is the *source* of our experience allows us to *notice* the quality of our thinking rather than *judge* it.

The Thought Cycle

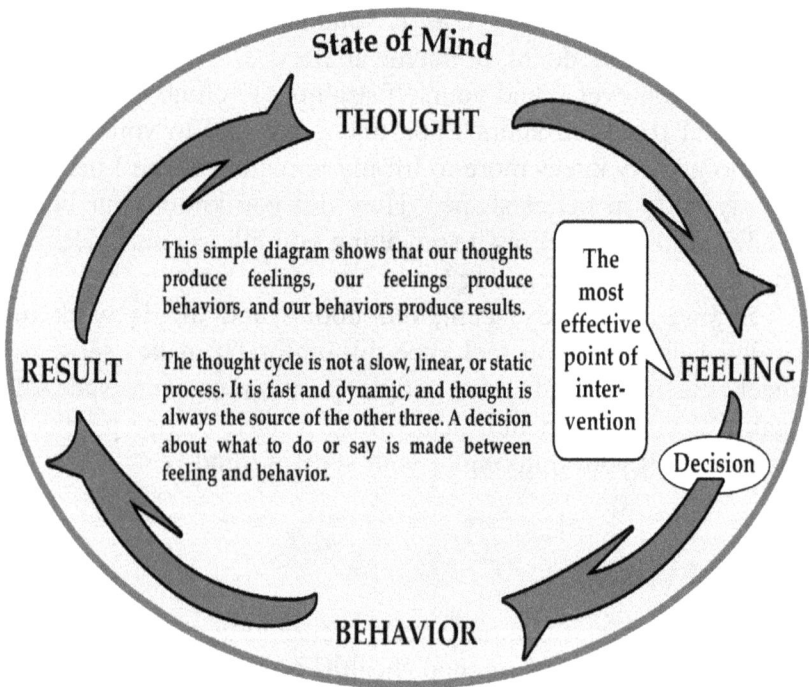

State of Mind

THOUGHT

This simple diagram shows that our thoughts produce feelings, our feelings produce behaviors, and our behaviors produce results.

RESULT

The thought cycle is not a slow, linear, or static process. It is fast and dynamic, and thought is always the source of the other three. A decision about what to do or say is made between feeling and behavior.

The most effective point of intervention

FEELING

Decision

BEHAVIOR

Key Points

The quality of the state of mind at the beginning of this cycle is crucial, because every step thereafter is cleansed or contaminated by the thoughts produced by it.

The cycle operates *continually* and always *within* state of mind.

Clear Thinking Produces:	Distracted Thinking Produces:
Inclusive feelings	Selfish feelings
Respectful behaviors	Adversarial behaviors
Focused results	Poorly accepted results

Four Elements of the Thought Cycle

Thought

- Thoughts constantly flow through the mind.
- The quality of thought moves back and forth along a continuum from mental clarity to mental distraction.
- Clarity is characterized by thinking that is more focused, organized, and responsive.
- Distraction is characterized by thinking that is more unfocused, disorganized, and reactive.

Feelings

- Feelings are the *direct manifestation* of the quality of thinking.
- Clarity produces feelings of openness, understanding, and compassion.
- Distraction produces feelings of judgment, arrogance, and fear.

Behaviors

- Clarity produces behavior that is specific, economical, precise, and swift.
- Distraction produces behavior that is unfocused, abrupt, too slow, and off target.

Results

- Clarity produces results that are more effective, sustainable, and aligned with purpose and goals.
- Distraction produces results that are shorter term, not as readily accepted, and may suffer from poor quality or the need for regular re-work. *(NOTE: The actual decision and result may be the same, but the wear, tear, and stress on people will increase.)*

How Does the Thought Cycle Relate to Leadership?

The traditional approach or focus of a leader is to intervene just *after* the behavior. At first glance, it may seem sensible. If you can adjust the behavior, you should get a different result. The problem is the quality of thinking that *produced* the behavior has not changed.

If you apply the thought cycle to our original scenario of discomfort while climbing, you can see that it doesn't matter if you need to adjust your body position or work on your conditioning; first you *think* about it to understand what you are trying to accomplish, then you get used to how it *feels*, then your *behavior* changes, and, finally, the *result* is different.

Whether we're trying to condition our bodies, listen to a client, or gain alignment on the Board of Directors, the same thought cycle is always in action. So, the next time you feel your thinking is off-kilter, just check the quality of your thought cycle. Round and round the cycle is okay, as long as you don't spin out of control.

Reflective Questions

What resonates with you in this chapter?

What surprises you about this chapter?

What are you curious to learn more about?

Bonus Question

What is an example of how you have noticed your thought cycle in action?

My Insights

CHAPTER THREE

Faith in Feelings

How do you know when you are on or off track with a response or decision? Have you ever heard someone say they trust their gut feelings? Have you ever had a feeling that what you were about to say was better left unsaid?

Feelings are the barometer, fragrance, and Richter scale of our thoughts. Pick any of those analogies or one of your own. The point is, we have a built-in physical and mental radar screen to let us know when we are on or off track—our feelings—and they are always eloquent in how they tell us the quality of our thinking.

When we feel pain, it lets us know if all our parts are in good working order. We don't get mad at the pain. Pain is a feeling. We pay attention to feelings because they give us important information about our natural state of well-being. They are evidence that our *physical radar screen* is in good working order.

> *Feelings are the barometer, fragrance, and Richter scale of our thoughts.*

Likewise, when we feel confused, angry, or downhearted, or in contrast when we feel lighthearted, decisive, or open-minded—*all* of these feelings are evidence that our *mental radar screen* is functioning properly.

Feelings are the *direct manifestation* of our thinking. Our thoughts produce feelings. Those feelings are the diagnostic output about the *quality of our thinking.* The quality of our thinking is our *state of mind.* Our state of mind fluctuates between being clear and distracted. Our feelings let us know which part of the continuum we are on.

Feelings are neither good nor bad. We don't have to *like* them to experience how useful they are. Most of us don't like pain, but we know the benefit of its presence.

So, how do we know what our feelings are telling us? What if we are trying to make an important decision? What if we are having a business discussion and are unsure of the approach to take? To make things simple, there are two easy feelings to keep in mind when trying to gauge if we are on a healthy thought track: Clear and Compelled.

Key Points—Notice if You are Feeling Clear

When You Are Clear, Your Thinking is Clear:

- Thoughts are organized, though not necessarily linear, and are relevant to the situation at hand. Your mind is open with enough perspective to receive and analyze the internal and external information you need to make clear decisions and take decisive action.

- You are able to listen without being judgmental or caught in a web of preconceived opinions.

- Relationships are smoother because you are more respectful, and you see more alternatives because you have a broader view.

- Though you may be physically and mentally active, you feel more energetic and can accomplish more with less time and effort.

Key Points—Notice if You are Feeling Compelled

When You Are Compelled, Your Thinking is Distracted:

- You may have strong opinions about a course of action, a greater sense of ownership for your ideas, or less patience with other approaches or people.

- You may engage in more persuasive or manipulative techniques to bring people to your point of view.

- Decisions and actions are either more prolonged or more reactive.

- You may feel fearful about how you are perceived, so the amount of worry in your mind increases.

- There is a greater sense of having energy drained but feeling a need to force your way through a situation.

- Relationships feel unsatisfying and full of effort. You may even experience the need to "fix" people.

Why Should We Have Faith in Feelings?

- They are innate and always present. We don't have to shop for them.

- They are universal. They are part of the human condition.

- They are the unfailing evidence of the quality of our thinking. Guaranteed.

- They are buoyant and will always return no matter how long or how often we try to suppress them.

- They are neutral. Neither good nor bad, feelings share important information with us so we can navigate life in a healthier way.

We've all experienced being clear and compelled—and we will again. Knowing that we can check our feelings to determine the quality of our thinking is a quick and easy remedy to become more patient with ourselves and others, make wise and timely decisions, establish better relationships, and experience less stressful mental wear and tear.

Reflective Questions

What resonates with you in this chapter?

What surprises you about this chapter?

What are you curious to learn more about?

Bonus Question

When have you noticed that awareness of your feelings helped you keep a clear mind?

What about a time when your lack of awareness took you down a path that was less effective than desired?

My Insights

CHAPTER FOUR

Mental Clarity—
Mental Distraction

Have you ever had a mesmerizing conversation with someone in the middle of a construction zone and been completely unaware of the noise? Have you ever gone to ponder a decision at your favorite spot in the park with no noise around and been unable to keep focused on the subject? Thoughts of everything *but* the topic intrude in your mind. Not only that, they keep bumping into each other in no particular order. It's like trying to herd gnats.

Those gnats are signs of mental distraction and are most noticeable when trying to make a decision. It doesn't matter what kind of decision. It could be about what car to buy, what business strategy to use, how to engage in relationships, what career to pursue, or how to live our lives. Our way of thinking permeates our entire life and every decision we will ever make.

Our thinking comes in two flavors: Clear and Distracted. Because we are human beings, we will taste both throughout life. Learning about the products of each type of thinking as it relates to decision making helps us recognize when we are on safe or shaky mental ground. And, *every* decision we *ever* make is affected by four key factors.

Four Key Decision Making Factors:

- **Personal Standards**: Our code of conduct that governs our sense of integrity.
- **Past Experience:** Any experience prior to the present moment about which we have knowledge. Examples include anything that has happened to us or others, historical events, and business practices.
- **Future Possibilities:** Anything imaginable that could happen in the future. It is the world of ideas, theories, dreams, and fantasies as applied to every aspect of life.
- **Cultural Norms:** Prevailing thoughts, behaviors, traditions, customs, and rituals believed in and practiced by any group of people anywhere. Cultural norms exist in families, groups of friends, schools, churches, communities, businesses, and nations.

Here are some thoughts about how these areas may look through the windows of Mental Clarity and Mental Distraction.

Personal Standards

Mental Clarity	Mental Distraction
• Leads us to consider if what we are about to do/decide will be congruent with our purpose, values, ethics, and reputation. • Respectful, responsive, and fair to all parties. • An appropriate use of time, talents, and abilities. • Willingness to accept accountability for the outcome even if it is not what we want.	• Leads us to focus on the satisfaction of our ego—self-image about how we currently view ourselves or want to be perceived. • We try to meet preconceived expectations about our roles and responsibilities. • An emphasis on winning at all costs, beating others, gaining power, assigning blame, and looking for revenge. • Our self-image may be *inflated* and manifest itself as arrogance, or *deflated* and manifest itself as shy, incapable, or unworthy. • We set expectations and limitations of who we can or cannot be, spend our lives trying to live up to them, and forget that we created them in the first place.

Past Experience

Mental Clarity	Mental Distraction
• We consider anything from the past as a valuable lesson that can be applied to the present and future. • We look at previous strategies and approaches with perspective to see what did not work well and take steps to avoid similar outcomes if possible. We also look at what did work well and make use of it in the future. • We consider risk-benefit options. • We understand the difference between learning from and appreciating the past.	• We worry about repeating mistakes or second-guess previous decisions. • We mourn "what might have been." • We defer living today while trying to re-enact the past. • We engage with people based on comparisons to people or situations in the past. • We live in the past or believe the past holds us hostage or determines our future.

Future Possibilities

Mental Clarity	Mental Distraction
• We review multiple scenarios with possible outcomes based on the best information available. • We gather other views and perspectives. • We remain flexible and open to new ideas or information. • We value a reflective state of mind that supports the capacity to dream, invent, innovate, and create.	• We get caught in a circular worry pattern about what might happen. • Worry is often mistaken for planning. • We become invested in a particular outcome based on personal preference without listening to or seeking other perspectives. • We have so much anticipation of how something will be that we are unable to be "present" for how it actually is.

Cultural Norms

Mental Clarity	Mental Distraction
• We understand habitual behaviors are evidence of habitual thought patterns. • We see our habits and those of others with interest and perspective. • We value learning and understanding the thinking behind traditions. • We consider the blend of other cultures as beneficial and enriching.	• We judge others as suspect, wrong, or flawed because their traditions and beliefs are different from our own. • We assume that because we were taught to be a particular way, it is not possible or desirable to change. • We use our powers of persuasion or coercion to change others to be like us.

Key Points—Mental Clarity—Mental Distraction

- Mental Clarity is not contingent on geography, time, or surroundings. Our greatest distractions are mental rather than physical.

- How busy the mind is has nothing to do with how busy the body is. The quieter the mind, the more efficient the mind *and* the body.

- Our natural state of mind is clear. We have to exert effort to maintain our distracting thoughts.

- Feelings of fear and judgment in relation to expectations about ourselves and others are the best indicators of being in a distracted state of mind.

- When mentally distracted, we often feel compelled to take impulsive action or to try to persuade others to be more like us.

- Worry is a habit of thought that has been learned and can be reduced significantly. There is no "healthy" amount of worry, so the desire would be to eliminate it from our mental diet. It serves no useful purpose and wastes a significant amount of time and energy.

- Once we know the feeling of Mental Clarity, Mental Distraction is more recognizable, becomes less tolerable, and is easier to dismiss.

Why is this Helpful to Know?

Thinking clearly is not a matter of force, strength, will-power, or external conditions. It's helpful to know the chatter in our minds is just a parade of thoughts. It's even *more* helpful to know we have a built-in radar system to detect the nature and usefulness of those thoughts. That radar system is our feelings.

How we *feel* lets us know if those thoughts are energizing clarity or draining distraction.

Mental Clarity and Decision Making

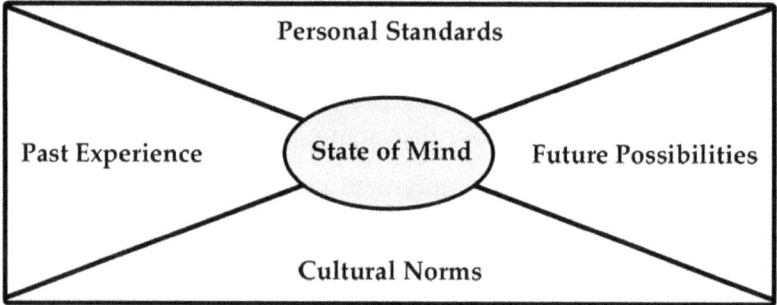

Personal Standards

Past Experience   State of Mind   Future Possibilities

Cultural Norms

Mental Distraction and Decision Making

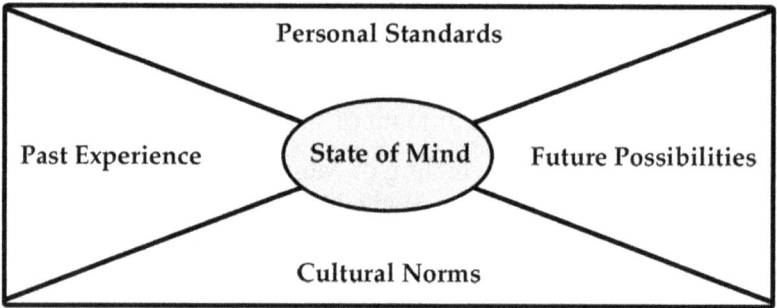

Personal Standards

Past Experience   State of Mind   Future Possibilities

Cultural Norms

Reflective Questions

What resonates with you in this chapter?

What surprises you about this chapter?

What are you curious to learn more about?

Bonus Question

What patterns of distraction seem most and least prevalent for you? What patterns of clarity seem most and least prevalent for you?

My Insights

CHAPTER FIVE

Innate Human Capacities

S ometimes you're hot and sometimes you're not. When you're *hot* you seem plugged into some transformative energy vortex filled with wisdom, creativity, intelligence, and vision. When you're *not* you feel lucky to be able to rub two thoughts together.

The truth is we all travel along that continuum every day of our lives. Sometimes we just spend more time at one or the other end of the spectrum. At the "hot" end, the mind is clear. At the "not" end, the mind is distracted.

> *Everyone has a natural inclination to have a clear mind. We have an innate understanding that a clear mind produces better ideas and results.*

Everyone has a natural inclination to have a clear mind. Have you ever heard anyone say, "I can't talk about such an important topic until my mind is more cluttered"? We have an innate understanding that a clear mind produces better ideas and results.

We have innate capacities, installed at birth, that are fully engaged when we are "hot." When we are "not", the capacities don't go on vacation. They are still there ready to serve. We just can't see them as well because we've pulled a mental curtain over them called mental distraction.

Key Points—Innate Capacities

Organized Thought:

Not necessarily sequential or linear, it is the product of our ability to process multiple and complex sources of mental and sensory information simultaneously in a way that is comprehensive and practical.

Analysis:

Process information in multiple ways; identify; compare; contrast; select options and alternatives; and create a logical pattern for decision-making or problem resolution. Personal intellect is a factor in our ability to analyze.

Memory:

A mental storage system for remembering any intellectual or sensory information. Memory is non-selective about what is stored and includes what we have directly experienced as well as what we have overheard, read, or seen. It has practical utility for daily living. Once we learn something it is stored for future use, so we don't need to re-learn our name, what our best friend looks like, or how to drive each day.

Creativity:

Our ability to innovate, invent, create new products and approaches to meet needs, solve problems, and express ideas.

Insight:

Sometimes called an "AHA!" moment, an insight is a spontaneous, new understanding that appears out of nowhere and frequently without actively thinking about it.

Key Points—Innate Capacities (continued)

Once an insight occurs, we *see* things differently and, therefore, *do* things differently.

Perspective:

A view of the bigger picture. It allows us to see an entire system including its segments and how they interact. Perspective allows us to have distance from our own thinking *while it is occurring,* understand others' points of view, set priorities, and understand that each of us experiences a separate reality.

Wisdom:

The ability to discern an approach characterized by clarity, health, respect, connection, and in the best interests of all. Wisdom is not contingent upon age, gender, religion, or personal intellect.

Common Sense:

The practical action component of wisdom. Once an approach has been determined, common sense lets us select the most appropriate actions to be employed.

Reflection:

The ability to consider or ponder information without actively concentrating on an outcome. Reflective thought is not limited by time and allows us to be responsive to need rather than reactive to circumstance. Much as the body rests and refreshes itself during sleep, reflection allows the mind to rest and refresh itself from levels of mental activity.

All Innate Capacities Are:

- Available to everyone
- Always operating harmoniously and simultaneously on a continuum
- Not sequential or hierarchical
- Products of a clear mind
- Accompanied by uplifting feelings such as goodwill, connection, and compassion.

So, what's not to like? Can you honestly think of a time in your life when you would *prefer to have less* wisdom, common sense, perspective, insight, reflection, memory, analysis, or creativity?

Why Aren't We Always at the Clear-Minded End of the Continuum?

- Because we are human, we experience mental distraction. It's not something to be ashamed of. It's just part of the human experience.

- The biggest distractions are thoughts of fear, worry, blame, attachment, and judgment, which create static in our connection to our other innate capacities. Unfortunately, those thoughts can appear compelling.

How Can We Re-Establish the Connection to Our Clear Mind?

- Let go of compelling thoughts by learning about and understanding the presence and value of the innate capacities and how they work.

- Consider examples of how they have presented themselves in your life. Think of examples of when you were "hot."

- Increase your awareness of your feelings and how they inform you about your state of mind.

- Become familiar with the feelings you notice when you are "hot" and when you are not.

- Make it a priority to understand the difference between innate and contingent. If your *internal* clear mind is contingent upon *external* circumstances or people, you relinquish your own well-being into the hands of others.

- Have you ever been in a situation in which others lost their bearings but you remained calm? The reason for the difference rests in the innate capacity for a clear mind rather than in the circumstance itself.

Why is This Helpful to Know?

These capacities are resident in *each* of us. And that means *you*. They are not reserved for what some of us might view as *special people*. What we call intuition, conscience, or inner voice, are just everyday evidence of listening to our innate wisdom. One person's genius is another person's common sense.

Understanding these capacities and how they work can change and equalize how we view ourselves and others. We become more tolerant, more inquisitive, more curious, more appreciative, and more grateful for the multiple ways in which we each manifest our capacities.

Here's the good news. Even after only reading this article, your awareness is already heightened. You will see examples of these capacities in your life—past and present. You will notice feelings associated with having a clear or distracted mind. And that *awareness* will help you see your thinking *in the moment* so you can more easily make adjustments.

And guess what? I predict you will be *hot* more often!

Reflective Questions

What resonates with you in this chapter?

What surprises you about this chapter?

What are you curious to learn more about?

Bonus Question

How have you experienced these innate capacities in your life? Describe.

My Insights

CHAPTER SIX

Innate Health

Our Default Setting

Innate health is an observation that the default setting for human beings is healthy psychological functioning. If people are left to their own healthy devices, they will automatically clear and quiet their minds. They will experience greater perspective and will be more astute about what their feelings tell them about their state of mind.

This is a major departure from other psychologies or models of personal growth, which assume people are "damaged goods" in need of repair. In those models we must struggle to "instill" healthy thinking, positive self-esteem, and creativity. Wisdom is reserved for geniuses. The best people can hope for is to become skilled at certain coping mechanisms to help them get through life.

The concept of innate health assumes that people are like corks in water—they have buoyancy. If the cork is tethered to the bottom of a tank, once cut loose it will rise to the surface. People may be tethered by insecure thoughts related to self image, ability, worth, judgment, fear, or worry. Once they quiet their minds, they recognize their thinking and the role those thoughts play in their experience of life. The default setting of innate health lets them rise to the surface where they have clear thinking and perspective on life and what it presents. Just like the cork, they have buoyancy.

Universal and Constant

Innate health is present in all people and available at all times. All we need to do is notice our feelings, which will tell us if our thinking is clear or distracted.

Our thinking is a dynamic rather than a static process. It is constantly flowing, and we respond to the quality of that thinking. When our thinking is distracted we experience more uncertainty and doubt. Those feelings are the internal expression of our distracted thinking.

When distracted, insecure thinking is released by the realization that "we are the thinker;" we experience our innate wisdom. We are able to "let go," feel less attached to our specific thoughts, and become more resilient. The wisdom was always there—we just pulled the curtain of distraction over it.

While everyone has the potential to realize their innate health, there is no guarantee that everyone will do so in their lifetime. However, the possibility is always present for anyone, at any level of understanding, at any time in their lives. The realization of innate health may be gradual or spontaneous.

The Psychological Immune System

Look at innate health in another way: as a psychological immune system. Our bodies have a physical immune system that helps us heal naturally. There is nothing we must do. If we cut our finger, left alone, the finger will heal. If the cut is minor, it may heal without leaving evidence there was ever anything wrong. If we get a cold, given time, our white blood cells will rally to help fight infection, and we will return to our original healthy state. If our thoughts are insecure, once our mind clears, we will return to our naturally healthy state of thinking.

The message of hope is that nothing needs to be added to us to allow us to live full, healthy, creative, productive, enjoyable lives. Everything needed is already present. All we need to do is notice and clear away the distractions.

Reflective Questions

What resonates with you in this chapter?

What surprises you about this chapter?

What are you curious to learn more about?

Bonus Question

What is an example of when you realized your own innate health?

How could you strengthen your own Psychological Immune System?

My Insights

CHAPTER SEVEN

Healthy High Performance

Overview

The business community is always focused on results. These results are often expressed as profit-loss, ROI, EPS, and industry-specific organizational metrics. All businesses, and the people who engage in them, want to achieve high performance.

There is a common perception that high performance requires a high price to be paid in terms of individual and group relationships at work and at home. Rarely considered is that high performance results can be achieved in a healthy environment. It is assumed they are mutually exclusive.

Our reservoir of innate health and resilience allows us to experience healthy high performance, a completely different way of achieving results. It is predicated on the understanding that when people are operating from a healthy state of mind, a clear mind, they will naturally be responsive to situational need, creative in their decisions, respectful of the views and contributions of others, and actively engaged in all aspects of their lives.

Most people have the fundamental understanding that the state of mind they are in has a direct impact on the quality of their performance and results. However, it is a common *misunderstanding* that the state of mind is controlled by outside circumstances and is, therefore, almost whimsical in its stability. People who seem to maintain their bearings under difficult circumstances are considered to be special.

Healthy high performance is a product of a clear mind and is governed by the same three principles previously discussed: the foundational understanding that *all* people have the capacity to live productive, happy lives and maintain their bearings regardless of the circumstances and situations they encounter. It is in this healthy state of mind that people have the maximum potential to optimize results.

Healthy High Performance in Business

I can't tell you how many CEOs and senior teams have told me they want more creativity, innovation, accountability, and alignment in their organizations. They want meetings that are focused and results oriented, yet allow for creative discussion. They want relationships that are collaborative, open-minded, trusting, respectful, and productive. They want to get rid of silo thinking. They want the collective organization to keep the bigger picture in mind. They want the workforce to be engaged and loyal.

Healthy High Performance is a strategic advantage because it sets you apart from the competition.

At the same time, people are already working hard, long hours, are feeling fried, and don't really have much company spirit left. They are sacrificing home life for corporate needs. So, senior leadership would like their people to have greater balance. As a matter of fact, the C-Suite would like more balance as well. Is it possible?

If a picture paints a thousand words, let's look at this one.

A Picture of a Healthy High Performance Organization

- High activity environment—yet a sense of calm.

- People seem to enjoy themselves and co-workers.

- There is a sense of fun, joy, accomplishment, fulfillment, and contribution in their work.

- When a serious problem appears, the knee-jerk response is to reflect to understand the needs rather than react by jumping to conclusions based on previous opinions, behaviors, or solutions.

- Change is viewed as the norm, an opportunity to learn, and an adventure.

- People have a sense of humor about circumstances, themselves, and others.

- People are considerate of each other when someone loses their bearings. They give each other the benefit of the doubt.

- Individuals and teams will not look for decisions until they have cleared their minds.

- Work seems active and vital instead of frenzied or stressful.

- People seem happy about the work they do and no need is seen for external motivation.

- New jobs, challenges, and responsibilities are met without fear and learned with a quiet, clear mind.

- Less effort exerted seems to yield greater results.

- People seem naturally to live balanced lives and don't feel the need for others or structures to keep them in balance.

Invariably, leaders begin to mentally salivate. However, the image, as appealing as it is, seems to go against everything they have previously thought possible. Can an organization be both healthy *and* high performing? Aren't they mutually exclusive characteristics? Let's take a look at the common assumptions about high performance.

The Traditional View of High Performance

- The thinking employed is derived primarily from memory; new ideas are rearranged from the past.

- Work requires much stress and effort, no pain no gain.

- There is a belief that high performance will naturally take a toll on health, family, and relationships. A price is expected and must be paid.

- Some coercion is necessary, and desirable, to get results.

- You get more from people when pressure and stress is increased.

- Mechanisms are required to get results.

- Extra hours, calls, trips, quotas, motivational programs, incentives, and artificial deadlines are necessary.

- There are consequences—health, relationships and, eventually, results suffer.

- Coping mechanisms are required and possibly offered or taught, but they actually add more stress.

- Busy people in business don't have the luxury to take time out to get a clear mind.

The Role of State of Mind

I haven't found anyone yet who doesn't believe that the state of mind we are in "influences" the quality of our actions and results. I go a giant step further. I believe it "determines" the quality of our actions and results. Everything we do, every decision we make, is a product of the state of mind we are in when we do it or make it. If the quality of our thinking, our state of mind, is clear, we make clearer, more relevant, wise, and timely decisions. When our thinking is distracted by fear, judgment, and competition, we either procrastinate or over-react so quality of product and relationships suffer.

The Power of a Clear Mind View of Healthy High Performance

- The thinking is fresh, using memory as it is relevant to the present.
- Clear thinking, a quiet mind, and reflection are valued as a means of unleashing creativity.
- There is greater humility, vision, patience, vitality, and productive speed instead of frenzy or laziness.
- Respect others and assume they want to do a good job; see reduction of stress as helpful to thinking.
- People know the difference between themselves and their work.
- There is a willingness and desire to explore possibilities rather than reverting to pre-conceived answers.
- No external mechanisms are required to assure results because people naturally do what is common sense to get the job done.
- Consequences: healthy, fulfilling relationships at work and home; naturally live in a balanced way rather than

|| looking for external mechanisms and structures to
|| provide balance.

Coping mechanisms are not required; people notice when they get off track and make common sense adjustments.

Key Points—Healthy High Performance

<u>**Competitive Edge Resides in the Quality of Our Thinking**</u>

- Incentive programs, etc., can be fun as games but we need to remember that is all they are—a game—and you made up the rules. They are not a measure of who you are.

- Remember that incentive programs, awards, etc., are external mechanisms and cannot replace the innate self-esteem of every individual.

<u>**Healthy High Performance is a Strategic Advantage**</u>

- Being responsive, flexible, nimble, creative, wise, clear-headed, proactive, and anticipatory of need sets you apart from the competition.

<u>**Demystified Apparent Paradoxes**</u>

- Sustained high performance can be attained without stress and complexity.

- Timely, results-oriented leadership is possible without the use of coercion.

- Forgiveness, vision, and support are strategic benefits and priorities.

Key Points—Healthy High Performance (continued)

<u>**Demystified Apparent Paradoxes (continued)**</u>

- Healthy functioning is a means rather than an end and leads to balance.

<u>**Learning is Generalized**</u>

- The leverage of the Power of a Clear Mind has a synergistic effect resulting in an exponential gain/benefit.

- There is a spillover benefit throughout life—there will be healthy high performance in all areas of life, including relationships.

- Deeper feelings and spirit of healthy high performance include humility, vision, patience, and vitality.

<u>**Two Things Happen when an Individual Becomes Healthier in an Organization, Family, and Community.**</u>

- Sabotage—Others feel threatened and become suspicious—may think people aren't working, are lazy, or goofing off, not putting in as much time and effort as they are. Yet they get results, recognition, and more responsibility. It seems unfair.

- Health of the Helper Effect—People gravitate toward health, others calm down, begin to see new possibilities for achieving results, and synergy is the norm.

Senior Leadership Accountability

All of the desired characteristics of a healthy and productive organization are possible. None of them can be trained or forced. Characteristics are not decisions to be made or behaviors to be taught. They are insights to be realized.

The CEO and senior leaders are accountable for setting the vision and creating a culture that expects and allows employees to be nimble, creative, productive, and aligned toward the bottom-line needs of the organization. Leaders cannot develop others until they develop themselves. It gives the term "role model" an entirely new meaning. It means being vulnerable enough to embark on a path of personal and collective development, and being humble enough to make mistakes and learn from them. And courageous enough to make it a priority and do it in "public."

Senior leaders are the only people who can paint the picture of the organization they hope to sustain. Creating a Healthy High Performance organization begins with a leadership focus on creating a Healthy High Performance senior team. It's the only way the picture will come alive.

Reflective Questions

What resonates with you in this chapter?

What surprises you about this chapter?

What are you curious to learn more about?

Bonus Question

What elements of HHP would you like to develop further in yourself? Your team/organization?

How would HHP be a strategic advantage for your company in your community?

My Insights

The Power of a Clear Mind—
The Experience

CHAPTER ONE

The Power of Insight

Do you remember your first insight? Was it helpful? How did it affect the way you live? Most of us would be hard pressed to remember the content of most of our insights let alone the first, but we probably remember the feeling. Often referred to as an "Aha!" moment people report insights as feeling fresh, surprising, coming out of the blue, and crystal clear.

The clarity is present because we have "seen" something inside us we had overlooked before. Have you ever used a flashlight to look in a dim closet and found something that surprised you? It's not because it wasn't there before. You just couldn't see it because the lighting was poor or you didn't think to look there in the first place. Having an insight is literally like a light turning on in a murky corner of your mind.

When the light turns on in our mental closet, we see our thoughts in a new way. Answers to questions and solutions to problems come to us when we are not actively engaged in thinking about them.

Our capacity to have insights is more important than the content of them.

Insights are original thought. You may have had the same idea before, or others may have come up with an identical idea. But, when you experience an insight, it is *new*. You see it *differently* than you did before. It is original to you in that moment.

Key Points—The Power of Insight

Practical and Profound:

- The reason we don't remember all our insights is because they are the natural product of a clear mind and occur so frequently we don't stop to take notice—especially of the "small" ones.

- Profound insights have an impact on how we live our lives in the long term.

- Practical insights help us make multiple decisions in our daily lives.

Prerequisites for Insights:

- An open, curious, reflective state of mind.

- Interest and willingness to see another view.

- Faith that other possibilities exist.

- Humility.

Sustained Change:

- Insights come from within. They cannot be externally applied or installed. Someone else's insights are useful information, but will have no lasting impact on our lives unless we have our own insight.

- A fundamental shift in thinking occurs so we *see* things differently.

- Because we *see* things differently, we *do* things differently.

Key Points—Characteristics of Insights

- Are accompanied by a fresh, uplifting, grateful feeling even if our new understanding sheds an unflattering light on our previous actions.

- Our shift in understanding may not become clear immediately. Insights are often noticed more in retrospect than in the moment.

- Are in *relation* to something else and are different than good ideas or decisions.

- We may think exercising is generally a good idea so we make a decision to go to a gym. The implementation of the decision requires effort and willpower. The result is often a back-slide.

- If we have an insight about exercise being *directly related* to our personal well-being and overall health, we are likely to increase exercise in our lives in ways that we will maintain.

- Are pervasive and permanent.

- Once we have an insight, our previous thinking no longer seems relevant.

- Reverting to prior behavior patterns indicates different behaviors have been *practiced* rather than naturally employed due to an insight.

- Are natural and available to everyone.

- Insights are not contingent upon age, gender, physical ability, circumstances, or intellect.

- Provide a compass for decision making and behavior by eliciting questions that promote reflection rather than accusations that provoke guilt.

What Would Life Be Like Without our Capacity for Insights?

Stagnant, stationary, and unfulfilling. Sound fun?

It's impossible to imagine a life without the possibility of learning, seeing other sides of a viewpoint, or having a broader understanding about ourselves and others.

Our *capacity* to have insights is *more important* than the content of them. Once we understand the practical purpose of insights and the natural way in which they occur, we can appreciate their power. Insights provide a mental staircase to the sky that gives us greater perspective about the world around us and the people in it. And we can climb that staircase without ever having to leave the comfort of our chairs.

Reflective Questions

What resonates with you in this chapter?

What surprises you about this chapter?

What are you curious to learn more about?

Bonus Question

What is an example of a personal insight you've had that you would consider practical? Profound?

What is an example of a professional insight you've had that you would consider practical? Profound?

My Insights

CHAPTER TWO

The Power of Perspective

Become the Observer of the Quality of Your Thinking

Perspective is all about Point of View. What is in front, behind, or around us depends upon where we stand. What we *see* depends on our willingness to open our eyes.

Nothing on our physical or psychological landscape is flat. We are presented angles, planes, and nuances. Our view shifts imperceptibly or radically based on how much we are willing to rotate.

No matter how much we shift our position, the landscape remains the same. Our *view* of the landscape is all that has changed.

The Gift of Perspective

Have you ever stood in front of a painting and felt yourself drawn into the depths of the rooms, corners, and crevices portrayed? Did you want to peek behind the red velvet curtain? Have you ever had

With perspective, we not only see the big picture, we see the whole picture.

to step back until a painting came into clear focus? Have you ever wondered how a flat canvas with globs of paint and bumpy brush strokes could evoke deep feelings or stimulate curiosity in you?

The answer to those questions lies in Perspective; a technique used by artists to convey multiple dimensions on a flat surface. Perspective is our internal artist. The closer we stand to the picture we are painting about the circumstances in our lives, the less we see of the bigger picture.

Distance and Humor—Two Key Elements of Perspective

Distance

Distance allows us to become an impartial observer of our circumstances.

We can see in the front, side, and rear view mirrors of what we are thinking *simultaneously*. We can step away from our own painful thinking. Perspective is like a friend pulling us back from a fire we didn't know was nearby.

Our thought habits become clearer to us. We can actually *catch* ourselves worrying, being judgmental, or obsessing on a problem.

We begin to see the *validity* of other views about us, our circumstances, how to make a decision, or solve a problem, without necessarily abandoning our own views or opinions. It becomes possible for us to understand that our positions, opinions, and *dearly* held beliefs may not be serving us well. We become curious about other approaches and ideas.

Perspective is also an antidote to the poison of arrogance. We have the presence of mind to call upon others because we see the value of their expertise and contributions in developing a more creative solution to any dilemma we face.

At a point when tight purse strings were required, the award-winning actress, Geraldine Page, once painted the front of her house yellow and left the other three sides a graying white. Her reason? Because that's all people could see from the road. It wasn't until people walked *around the path* that they could see how the house really looked. The yellow house on the hill was Geraldine's illusion.

The distance perspective provides allows us to see the *entire* picture—not just the limited illusion we've allowed ourselves or others to see.

Humor

Humor is the great equalizer. A sense of humor lets us take ourselves less seriously. We can see irony and absurdity.

I saw a play recently, a memoir wherein the actress said, "If my life wasn't funny, it would just be true—and that would be unacceptable." She was talking about how her sense of humor helped her navigate some very difficult times in her life.

When we can see the humor in our past and current predicaments and reactions, it takes the sting away. Haven't you laughed later about an incident you didn't find very amusing at the time?

When we put our sense of humor in a drawer, we tend to see ourselves as magnets for adversity. Our *own* troubles are clearly the worst and we begin singing, "Nobody Knows the Troubles I've Seen" to anyone within earshot. Perspective allows us to see the difficulties of others in *relation* to our own through the soft-focus lens of compassion instead of through the eyes of comparison and judgment.

Here's my definition of adversity: **Adversity is anything that isn't going the way I want it to.**

The ability to see the humor and humanity in our circumstances is *evidence* our thinking has cleared. When we are more lighthearted, we are in the best position to engage in what might otherwise be difficult dialogue, solve problems, and make important decisions that will affect our well-being.

Is This True in Business Too?

It's true in *any* situation in life. Business is no exception because business is *part* of life.

Is there a thorny issue to discuss or crucial strategic decision to make? Is there a relationship in need of mending? Is alignment needed for the team to achieve better results? When distance and humor are present in the room, it is the *best* time to tackle "difficult" issues to discover the *wisest* answer.

When your spirits lift it is safe to proceed.

The Power of Perspective

See the Big Picture

Our ability to see the big picture objectively allows us to learn and broadens our horizons. Our thinking is farsighted rather than myopic. We see options and possibilities. We engage the help we need with humility, respect, and without ego pangs of perceived weakness. We not only see the big picture, we see the *whole* picture.

See Systems

As we look at the bigger picture, we can see systems in action, and how each part of the system is related to the others. We make connections that simplify our approach to dealing with anything in our lives. Life is not a sequence of circumstances; it is a combination of circumstances occurring concurrently.

The London Underground is a good example. I worked in London for a few years and occasionally encountered visitors who were intimidated by the swirling mass of humanity. I would tell them to stand back and watch the flow for a while. What needed to be done and in what order gradually became clear. The distance they afforded themselves from their initial discomfort allowed them to become competent in, and unafraid of, navigating unfamiliar surroundings.

See Separate Realities

I've previously said the state of mind we are in determines what we make of, and how we react to, the circumstances in our lives. I also said a clear mind is the foundation of our ability to experience our psychological well-being and to keep our bearings, regardless of the severity or importance of our circumstances.

Let me state the obvious. We are *always* thinking. The quality of our thinking fluctuates. Sometimes we're clearer, and sometimes we're more distracted. Now here's the important part. So is everyone else!

Remember the use of perspective in painting? The painter creates perspective. We have perception—the ability to *see* perspective. Each of us has a different perception about what we see. No two people will see or experience the painting in the same way. Similar, perhaps, but not the same.

We live in separate realities. What I see is different than what others see. What is true for me is not true for everyone else. What I make of my circumstances is different from what someone else makes of similar circumstances. There is no *one* reality.

When we understand that separate realities exist, we give ourselves—and others—the benefit of the doubt. Perspective clarifies why someone else will think differently and come to different conclusions. Not right or wrong—just different.

Bottom Line

When perspective is present, we can breathe a sigh of relief. There is no need to judge or be judged. There is no fear because the stakes are high. There is no sense of struggle or doubt about our capacity to deal with whatever appears before us.

Reflective Questions

What resonates with you in this chapter?

What surprises you about this chapter?

What are you curious to learn more about?

Bonus Question

What is an example of perspective helping you see a bigger picture than you saw before?

What is an example of your ability to see separate realities without being judgmental?

My Insights

CHAPTER THREE

Reflective Thinking and Decisive Action

How do you know when to stop reflecting and take action?

Can you reflect and act simultaneously? How do clarity and decisiveness of action relate to depth of reflection?

The answers may become more apparent as you imagine these scenarios:

- An average citizen quickly responds to victims at the scene of an accident.

- A young child suddenly pulls the plug from the outlet of a machine that is emitting sparks.

- A man on an assembly line rapidly repairs a pipe in danger of causing a gas leak.

In all three scenarios the people were operating in a state of mind called reflective thinking. Reflective thinking is an innate capacity producing quick, focused, and economical action. In these scenarios all we *see* is the action. Because everyone reacts so quickly, it can appear there is no thinking occurring. In fact, thinking is *always* in motion. It is either clear or distracted.

Reflective thinking and decisive action are not mutually exclusive. In fact, they are mutually beneficial.

Reflective thinking and decisive action occur concurrently. You don't "do" them as a sequence. They are simultaneous. Decisive action is always a product of thought. Again, the distinction is whether the thinking is clear or distracted.

Distracted thinking produces unnecessary or unproductive activity, few clear priorities, and a feeling of panic. Clear thinking discerns importance and includes the perspective to assign priority of action based on urgency of need or leveraged benefit. Both will look busy because the action is seen, not the thinking.

How often, in times of stress, do you remind yourself to count to ten before doing or saying something? You've probably even advised others to, "Just calm down until you get your bearings back." That's your natural wisdom speaking to you and speaking to the natural wisdom in others. It's the pause that refreshes the mind. The minute you calm down, you've "activated" your reflective thinking capacity.

The important thing to remember is the capacity for reflective thinking is *always* available. So why just reserve it for stressful times? It's common sense to want to have your best thinking and wisdom available in any and every circumstance.

Key Points—Reflective Thinking and Decisive Action

- Reflective thinking is a manifestation of an *open* or *clear* state of mind. Therefore, reflective thinking is a *state of mind* rather than an *activity* to be performed.
- Reflective thinking and decisive action are not mutually exclusive. In fact, they are mutually beneficial.
- Decisive action has everything to do with clarity of thinking and nothing to do with speed. Never confuse speed of action with speed of thought.
- In a clear state of mind, options and alternatives are more apparent, complex data are more easily analyzed, and extraneous information is more quickly discarded.
- Reflective thinking allows you to consider your actions and change your mind as appropriate, increasing your flexibility and responsiveness.
- There is no guarantee you will like the outcome of your actions, but you will have operated at your optimum capacity during the process.

Reflective Questions

What resonates with you in this chapter?

What surprises you about this chapter?

What are you curious to learn more about?

Bonus Question

What is an example of when you employed reflective thinking and decisive action in a difficult or stressful situation?

My Insights

CHAPTER FOUR

The Neutrality of Events

Have you ever known someone whose car was stolen, who suffered a serious illness, or lost their job? How did they handle it? Were they undone by it? Did they view it as the worst thing that could happen? Did they ask, "Why me?" Did it ruin their day, week, year, life?

Have you ever known someone who experienced the same kinds of situations yet were able to deal with the consequences, learn from them, let go, and move on? Have you ever known someone who actually found some *appreciation* for the situation in retrospect?

> *A clear mind allows us to deal with any event life provides—it also allows us to learn, let go and move on.*

What accounts for the difference in reactions to the same or similar events? The difference is the state of mind in which they *experience* the event and/or the memory of the event.

Stuff Happens—Letting Go and Moving On
(*Stuff: events, circumstances, situations, conditions, and people*)

No matter how much we like to think we are in control of our lives, we are not. Unforeseen things occur for which we are not prepared and would not have requested. Certainly, we can take responsible precautions. We can exercise and eat well, drive safely, choose our friends wisely, treat people with respect, be accountable for our results at work, and avoid swimming in shark-infested waters.

And yet, accidents occur, illness visits, and jobs disappear. Are these events good or bad?

Dominant Cultural View—Perceived

There is a dominant cultural view that some events are bad and others are good. The assumption is that there is universal agreement on the "badness" or "goodness" of the event. Another assumption is that there is universal agreement on what the natural or normal reaction to the event should be.

Distracted State of Mind View—Actual

Some reactions and responses to events appear to be common or frequent, but they are by no means universal.

The state of mind we are in *during* the event determines our reaction *to* the event.

When our state of mind is distracted—consumed with insecure, fearful, and judgmental thinking—we tend to find fault with the person or event and feel victimized as a result. It feels as though our response is contingent on external factors.

Elements of External Contingency

Time:

The event is in progress, occurred recently, or in the distant past.

Duration:

The situation or condition lasted a minimal or moderate period of time, or is permanent.

Proximity:

The event happened to you or people you know; you or people you know are affected by it; events happened to people or in places unknown to you.

Consider a flood. You may have been in it or affected by it, knew people who were in it or affected by it, read about it but knew nothing about the people affected or the place where it occurred.

Severity:

The situation or condition may be annoying, inconvenient, disastrous, life threatening, or fatal to you, someone you know, or people unknown to you.

For some people an event gradually loses its sting as time progresses. This accounts for another bit of conventional wisdom—"time heals all wounds." Yet many people carefully nourish their grudges for a lifetime.

It isn't time, duration, proximity, or severity that heals. It is the shift in quality of thinking *about* any event or situation that gives perspective and changes perception.

Results of External Contingency

- If the event is at "fault" for misery, there is an implied debt owed, which breeds a desire for retaliation, retribution, and revenge.

- Satisfaction is usually not achieved, and there is an escalating desire and demand for further punishment.

- Personal well-being appears to be contingent upon forces and sources external to us and beyond our control.

- Focus on fault, blame, and revenge is actually an obstacle to recovery, healing, and repair of relationships.

Clear State of Mind View

Have you ever noticed some people seem to maintain their bearings regardless of the event they experienced? They are often viewed as unusual. Perhaps they possess some special qualities, don't have normal human feelings, are robotic, don't really care, or maybe they *are* upset but are skilled at *appearing* calm.

I repeat. The state of mind we are in *during* the event determines our reaction *to* the event.

When our state of mind is clear, our innate health is in full operation. We are responsive to need, creative, decisive, and have the perspective to know what to do, and how and when to do it.

When personal or professional stakes are high, which state of mind would you like to prevail— clear or distracted?

Elements of External Contingency

Guess what? There aren't any. There is no sense of internal contingency on external sources. There is an understanding that a sense of well-being is not caused, determined, or governed by anything or anyone external to us.

Results of Clear State of Mind View

A clear state of mind yields greater clarity, focus, flexibility, and creativity in dealing with, and making decisions about, the event and its consequences.

- Appropriate, relevant action will be taken to serve justice rather than vengeance.

- Recognize that there is no universal reaction to any event.

- Understand that reactions to, and levels on contingency experienced by, events are solely determined by our state of mind.

- Recovery, healing, and repair of relationships are not only seen as possible, they become a priority.

Bottom Line

When personal or professional stakes are high, which state of mind would you like to prevail—clear or distracted? I vote for clarity!

The fact is, each of us has lost our bearings from time to time—and we will again. It is also true that each of us has *maintained* our bearings in trying circumstances—and we will again. We are human beings, and we will experience insecure thoughts and secure thoughts. Knowing the difference between them and understanding their source is important.

It is a clear mind that allows us to deal with any event life provides *while* maintaining a balanced perspective. Our natural resilience allows us to learn from the experience without feeling victimized by it. A clear mind allows us to let go and move on.

STUFF HAPPENS
Letting Go and Moving On

Elements of External Contingency

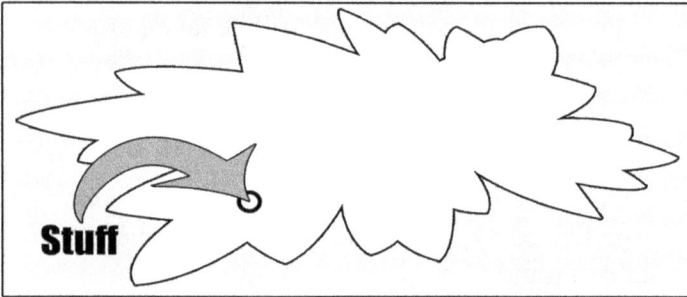

Time
Now
Recent Past
Distant Past

Duration
Minimal
Moderate
Permanent

Proximity
In it
Know People in it
Affected by it
Know People Affected by it
Unknown People/Places Affected by it

Severity
Annoyance
Inconvenience
Disaster
Life Threatening
Fatal

Stuff Happens—Letting Go and Moving On

Dominant Cultural View (Perceived)

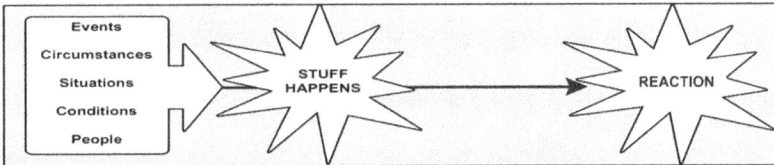

Distracted State of Mind View (Actual)

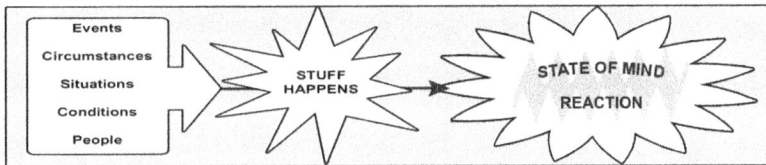

Result

- Assumed universal reaction directly linked to the event.

- Attribution of feelings and actions to the event.

- If the event is at "fault" for misery, there is an implied debt owed, which breeds a desire for retaliation, retribution, and revenge.

- Satisfaction is usually not achieved, and there is an escalating desire and demand for further punishment.

- Personal well-being appears to be contingent upon forces and sources external to us and beyond our control.

- Focus on fault, blame, and revenge is actually an obstacle to recovery and healing.

Stuff Happens—Letting Go and Moving On

Clear State of Mind View

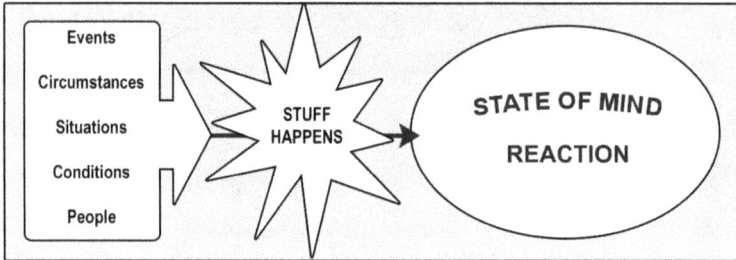

Events
Circumstances
Situations
Conditions
People

STUFF HAPPENS

STATE OF MIND

REACTION

Result

- Greater clarity, focus, flexibility, and creativity in dealing with, and making decisions about, the event and its consequences.

- Appropriate, relevant action will be taken to serve justice rather than vengeance.

- Recognize that there is no universal reaction to any event.

- Understand that reactions to, and levels of contingency experienced by, events are solely determined by state of mind.

- Recovery and healing are not only seen as possible, they become a priority.

Reflective Questions

What resonates with you in this chapter?

What surprises you about this chapter?

What are you curious to learn more about?

Bonus Question

What is an example of a time you and another person had very different views of an event in which you were both involved? When did you see that or another event as neutral?

My Insights

CHAPTER FIVE

Thought Recognition

Thought recognition is the degree to which we see the role and function of thought as the source of creating our reality. It has nothing to do with the content of our thoughts.

The function and role of thought is common to all people much as the function and role of the cardiovascular system is common to all people.

Levels of Thought Recognition

Passing Thought—Neutral—No Attachment

‖ • May be considered—throw away thoughts.

Preferences and Desires—Low Attachment

‖ • Easy to change your mind.

Ideas/Opinions—Moderate Attachment

‖ • These seem more important, but you can still let go.

Beliefs/Point of View/Values—Strong Attachment

- You hold these thoughts dear, such as political and religious beliefs, human and animal rights, etc.
- Beliefs are simply a cluster of thoughts arranged in a way that makes sense to you.
- You are aware and can accept that others hold different beliefs.
- Tendency to try to persuade others to your view.

Convictions—Significant Attachment

- Your self-image, self-concept is attached.
- Views about morals, ethics, etc.
- You know others have different views, but they are wrong.
- Militant views and approach.

Mental Habits/Habitual Thinking—Significant Attachment

- Familiar insecure thoughts but they don't seem like thoughts. They seem like natural things for humans.
- Worry, stress, anger, resentment, judgment, and phobias are examples of mental habits and habitual thinking.

Reality—Complete Attachment

- The way it is! There is no possibility it is related to thought.
- This level is the hardest to recognize.

The Role of Feelings

- Our feelings are reactions to our thoughts and serve as a barometer to the quality of our thinking. Feelings are the built-in warning system we each have to alert us to the health of our state of mind.

- Because we are not aware of each thought we have, the way we "catch" them is in how they manifest as feelings.

More on Mental Habits

- Thought habits are in and of themselves addictive. They may not feel good to us, but they are familiar.

- When our thought habits are painful, we may resort to a variety of behaviors such as jogging, shopping, abusing various substances, etc., to help us feel better not realizing that our thinking is the creator of the pain. The object is to get away from the painful thoughts.

- When we don't recognize that it is our thinking that creates our joy *and* our pain, we may believe it is the external object or behavior (jogging, shopping, abusing substances, etc.) that provides the relief.

- As our understanding of the role of thought deepens, our belief that we need to rely on external "escapes" diminishes and goes away.

Profiles in Thought Recognition

High Level of Thought Recognition

Life generally feels effortless and natural. People are able to keep their bearings in times of stress, and experience deep feelings much of the time. It is understood that a clear mind produces insights that are practical and profound in daily life, and no coping mechanisms for stress are needed. Living in this state seems ordinary. Untoward circumstances will occur, but the ability to navigate them with ease is determined by the quality of thinking. The source of peace, comfort, and joy is internal and non-contingent.

Moderate Level of Thought Recognition

Personal and professional relationships are stable. However, life is seen as requiring effort, and relationships and work have a built-in stress level. Multiple and varied coping mechanisms are needed. The world is full of obstacles and strong determination is needed to overcome them. Energy is expended driving toward external measures of success and reward. The source of peace, comfort, and joy is external and contingent on circumstances.

Lower Level of Thought Recognition

Personal and professional life is reasonably stable, but with a high level of dissatisfaction. Untoward circumstances are seen as crisis; others are seen as the cause of difficulty. Judging, blaming, and complaining are primary coping mechanisms. Peace, comfort, and joy may enter your life, but they are suspect, fleeting, contingent on circumstances, and not generally part of the "real world."

Minimal Level of Thought Recognition

Life is one crisis after another. Acting-out behavior, violence, drugs, or other addictions may be ways of coping with the overwhelming pressures of life. In more severe cases institutionalization may be required.

In Contrast to Moods

- Moods are an observation that the quality of our thinking fluctuates over time. We may notice being light-hearted or downhearted over a period of time. These clusters of feelings will come and go forever. It is part of the human experience.

- Levels of Thought Recognition do not fluctuate up and down. They are permanent until another insight produces an upward shift.

- When we have a High Level of Thought Recognition we still experience the full range of our moods. However, we recognize that our current state of mind is at the root of the mood state we happen to be in.

- When in a low mood, there is no need to do anything other than recognize it for what it is. Like the weather, it will change.

Bottom Line

Understanding thought recognition is the key to permanent change.

As you have insights about the role of thought in life, your level of understanding increases. That upward shift is permanent. You can only continue to gain understanding or stay stable. You cannot lose your understanding.

An increased level of understanding is accompanied by increased perspective. The shift is internal and insight-based rather than contingent on external circumstances.

Any topic will look different to us depending on the degree to which we recognize thought. For example, consider the topic of respect. At a lower level of understanding, respect is something that has to be earned and is contingent upon what others do or don't do, say or don't say.

When viewed from a high level of understanding, respect is easy and natural to give and receive. It is understood that it is not contingent upon the actions or behaviors of self or others. Respect, like most characteristics, is not something we *do*; it's something we *live*.

Thought recognition can only occur in a clear mind. Because of the innate resilience and buoyancy of a clear mind, every shift in understanding is an insight that increases in breadth and depth and will push to emerge through any opening it can find. As with all insights, it may be unsettling, is often surprising, but always inspiring.

Reflective Questions

What resonates with you in this chapter?

What surprises you about this chapter?

What are you curious to learn more about?

Bonus Question

What are some examples of thoughts/opinions you have and where would you place them on the levels of thought recognition?

My Insights

CHAPTER SIX

Organizational Immune System

Healthy Organizations are Comprised of Healthy Individuals

When was the last time you had a physical exam? Dental exam? Your car tuned? Your computer examined for viruses? Renewed your car or home insurance? Took your animal to the vet? Weeded your lawn? Reviewed your budget and financial plan? Put batteries in smoke alarms?

When was the last time you focused on your psychological health and well-being? Engaged in personal or professional development opportunities beyond subject matter expertise? Looked at the quality of your personal and professional relationships? Questioned the source and quality of your opinions and beliefs?

When was the last time you wondered when I would stop barraging you with questions?

I've always found it fascinating that people pay more attention to their bodies and belongings than they do to their minds. I'm not talking about education and training in knowledge, skills, and competencies. I'm talking about the quality of the thinking that governs how they *engage* in learning and employing the knowledge, skill, and competency.

Organizations are a prime example. They have huge budgets, a large workforce, and corporate reputations on the line. Yet many are severely deficient in focusing on the development of the key element that creates a culture of creative engagement in the business. That key element is the quality of thinking—the state of mind—of those who are producing the product, spending the money, and managing the relationships that create the corporate reputations.

The final accountability rests squarely on the shoulders of senior leadership. And, in my experience, they are not unaware of the issue or their accountability. While there are those who don't see the link between culture and results, or merely pay lip service to it, most leaders genuinely want to make a cultural shift. They simply don't know how to start, what to focus on first, or how to keep an eye on results at the same time. It feels like trying to shift the direction of the corporate ocean liner.

Taking an action, or changing a procedure, process, policy, or system can be deceptively appealing. The idea is that a simple change will make people work more efficiently and effectively. Maybe it will, but does it change the "atmosphere" of the workplace? There is the deception and the dilemma. Changing objective items does not change subjective forces. It is just a band-aid on a wound. The wound looks better, but it's still there.

Creating a Healthy Culture

The atmosphere is commonly known as the organizational culture. Culture is often described as "the way we do things around here." The "way" does not only refer to the policies, procedures, and systems, it also refers to the way people operate with each other—the way individual and collective relationships are viewed and conducted.

You can have a brilliant procedure, but if people are suspicious, resentful, disrespectful, unaligned, apathetic, or competitive with each other, the procedure is no better than the paper it is written on.

Most cultures are not so severely dysfunctional, but to the extent any of these characteristics exist to the point of frustrating relationships and results, they need to be addressed.

The place to look for an answer is not another procedure. It is the state of mind of the individuals and the organization. A culture is not just habits of behavior, but habits of thinking. At its core, culture is a compilation of thoughts unquestioned and agreed upon by a group of people.

Here's an extreme example. One department sees itself as the most important part of a company. It begins to view other departments with suspicion and irritation. They feel they don't get the financial and people resources or the recognition they deserve. They stop listening and talking to one another—or do so grudgingly. Silos are built and fortified, and turf is protected.

As I said, this is extreme, but the behaviors are commonly recognized. To the extent this situation is ignored or endured, it is at least tacitly accepted as the norm. It is part of the culture.

In all my years of experience, I guarantee you the problems most prevalent on the minds of leaders are "people problems." They certainly have strategic dilemmas, but the only way to deal with any strategy is through people.

Innate Health—Priority, Prevention, and Cure

When leaders don't pay attention to the collective organizational state of mind, decisions are often reactionary—fear based. There is a negative impact on the quality of performance and productivity at *every* level. Everything suffers—from financial stability, to management, workforce, and union relationships, to Wall Street reputations.

The deleterious effects also extend to the family. Leaders and members of the workforce are always talking about strained relationships at home and feeling pulled between organizational effectiveness and personal balance.

When leaders *do* pay attention to creating a clear-minded organizational state of mind—a healthy culture—silos disappear, people stop in-fighting and start listening, and they are more creative, innovative, responsive, wise, and decisive. There is greater alignment to corporate vision, strategy, and goals that essentially eliminates time-wasting arguments and lip service. Decision-making and problem solving are streamlined, accelerated, and sacred cows are put out to pasture.

The Power of a Clear Mind unleashes individual and collective innate health and strengthens the organizational immune system to create stability regardless of shifting priorities, as well as economic, technological, or political turbulence. A clear-minded organization is more flexible and nimble so there is greater readiness for an economic turnaround.

Leading from a clear mind doesn't mean you're exempt from problems. But, you can navigate them with greater wisdom and less physical and psychological wear and tear.

Problems are just problems. Events are just events. How well we deal with them is determined by our state of mind. And I think a clear state of mind is better than a distracted one.

How might results change if we placed as high a priority on our psychological and organizational immune systems as we do on the health of our bodies and the engines of our cars?

How might organizational results change if we placed as high a priority on assessing and strengthening our psychological and organizational immune systems as we do on the health of our bodies and the engines of our cars?

Reflective Questions

What resonates with you in this chapter?

What surprises you about this chapter?

What are you curious to learn more about?

Bonus Question

In what ways could your organizational immune system be strengthened? How and what could you contribute?

My Insights

The Power of Listening—
The Results

CHAPTER ONE

Preparing to Listen

When we decide to be leaders, we make a choice to be of service to people. Some of those people will be our employees and some will be our clients. Listening to them is not about steps or techniques, it's about presence. There is a naturally wise way to prepare to listen, which includes clearing our minds of our own debris so we are ready to receive what is on someone's mind.

Have you ever planted a tree without digging a hole? Tried to cook dinner without food in the house? Started driving before putting the car in gear? Run a marathon in loafers? Stood up from a chair without uncrossing your legs? Of course not! Preparation is just common sense.

Our daily lives are filled with countless acts of preparation. They seem invisible to us because they have become common sense. It seems normal that actors rehearse, athletes stretch, musicians practice, meetings have an agenda, and carpenters sharpen a saw.

We prepare so we can more easily accomplish our objectives.

Do we really have *objectives* when listening? If we intend to be valuable leaders, we'd *better*. One of the major complaints in any relationship is not feeling heard. And it has nothing to do with sound waves or eardrums.

What Does Listening Have to do With Leadership?

Organizations look to their leaders for perspective and hope. When those two elements are present, people feel *heard*. Feeling heard has nothing to do with agreement or getting one's way. When people feel heard, they begin to relax and their own perspective and hope automatically increase. They may also want expert advice, new ideas, or approval of a new strategy, but none of those things can occur effectively if the needs have not been heard.

For the leader, listening is an opportunity to learn. We want to learn not only *what* someone is thinking but, more importantly, *how* the person is thinking. The "how" is the quality of the *state of mind* (Clear or Distracted) from which he is reviewing his options, making decisions, solving problems, and relating to staff, colleagues, board members, or the community. His habitual state of mind (Clear or Distracted) is far more revealing and important than the circumstances themselves.

> *The best way to prepare to listen is to clear your mind, open your mind, and engage your mind.*

Pre-requisites for learning include humility, curiosity, interest, and reflection. What does *he* think the implications and consequences might be? What is *she* afraid of or proud of? What feelings would *he* like to experience more or less of? We want to hear how *she* views her situation, not get distracted by how *we* view it.

How Can We Prepare to Listen?

Leading from the Power of a Clear Mind includes standards of professionalism and respect. Those standards reside in the quality of the state of mind *we* bring to be of service to our people. All people have a need to be heard, so it is only professional and respectful to begin with preparing to listen.

Preparing to listen has nothing to do with our external environment and everything to do with our internal state of mind.

Key Points—Preparing to Listen

<u>**Clear Your Mind**</u>

A clear mind is like a blank sheet of paper. It is free of judgments, expectations, and prescriptions.

Clearing the clutter in your own mind is necessary to make space for what the employee or client has to say. Much as the farmer loosens the soil and clears it of debris so seeds can be planted, we need to clear our minds of the debris of preconceived opinions, mental distractions, beliefs, and opinions. If we don't clear our minds, the other person has to compete with *our* distractions to be heard.

<u>**Open Your Mind**</u>

An open mind has perspective to see connections and relationships in the entire picture, can discern relevant issues within the distortion of trivia, and has the humility to understand there is more to learn than what is already known. When our minds are open we create a safe zone comprised of trust, respect, and neutrality. We have willingness and a desire to learn.

Key Points—Preparing to Listen (continued)

<u>**Engage Your Mind**</u>

An engaged mind that is clear and open can be completely attentive to the concerns, needs, and the state of mind in which the other person is operating. Their best interests are dominant.

When the mind is engaged, we can synthesize the elements of what we have heard into a few key points to help someone turn down the volume on his own mental distractions. He can then discover the role *his* state of mind plays in the variety and quality of options perceived, decisions made, and relationships created.

Only when we have prepared to listen can we actually begin to Listen for Clarity. At that point, we are qualified to enter a respectful partnership and join our partner on a journey of discovery.

Prepare to listen. It's just common sense.

Reflective Questions

What resonates with you in this chapter?

What surprises you about this chapter?

What are you curious to learn more about?

Bonus Question

How often do you "prepare" to listen? How?

What was the difference in outcome between when you did and did not prepare to listen? Describe your state of mind in each case.

My Insights

CHAPTER TWO

Listening for Clarity

Once we've prepared ourselves to be fully engaged, we orient ourselves in the direction of what to listen "for." Paramount in our minds is listening for clarity about what is on someone's mind, including the level of clarity and distraction in their thinking. Our thinking needs to be clear of the rubble of preconceived agendas, actions, or answers.

Get Your Free Hearing Aids Here

On a scale of 1 to 10, how would you rate yourself as a listener? How would your employees, spouse or close friends rate you? Most of us claim to be good listeners, yet sometimes we're told we are good listeners about some topics but not others.

We all seem to have the ability to be superb *and* lousy listeners. What accounts for the difference? Do we all need hearing aids?

Yes, actually, just not the kind you can buy. The best hearing aids available are free. You already have the capacity to turn up the volume on your listening skills. All you need is Interest, Curiosity, and Reflection.

You have the capacity to turn up the volume on your listening skills. All you need is Interest, Curiosity, and Reflection.

Have you ever noticed how easy it is to listen to someone or something if you are interested in the subject? Have you noticed a continuing curiosity to learn more? Have you noticed you tend to reflect on what you have heard to be clear about its meaning or implications?

Interest, Curiosity, and Reflection are the key elements of listening for clarity. They are also part of the foundation for building and maintaining any relationship in your life.

Key Points—Listening for Clarity

<u>**Interest**</u>

- Is evidence of a desire to *know* more.

- Requires a clear, undistracted mind—clear of mental distractions, preconceived notions, hidden agendas, or any other thoughts that pull our attention from the current conversation or project.

- Assumes we have the best interests of the other person at heart.

- Provides a safe environment for someone to confide in and explore their thinking with us.

- Does not require prior knowledge or experience with the topic being discussed.

Key Points—Listening for Clarity (continued)

Curiosity

- Is evidence of a desire to *learn* more.

- Requires the willingness to enter and explore the "unknown."

- Is a product of humility. We cannot engage our curiosity if we believe we already know everything.

- Always contains an element of surprise.

- Is a prerequisite for being creatively responsive.

Reflection

- Is evidence of a desire to *understand* more.

- Gives us the perspective to see the "whole picture" by putting the pieces of a puzzle into a shape that is logical, organized, and clear.

- Allows us to see beyond what is apparent on the surface.

- Provides time and opportunity to see and explore peripheral issues and how they relate to the current topic.

- Illuminates the macro-view of any situation, circumstance, or habit of thought.

Listening is an iterative, dynamic process requiring full engagement with all parties. Listening for clarity using our hearing aids of Interest, Curiosity, and Reflection will always set both speaker and listener at ease. The safety zone created allows each person to see beyond previous assumptions.

Individual and mutual insights will result in approaches, solutions, and decisions that are more creative and sustaining, because each person *sees* previous circumstances in a *new* way.

Having once experienced the benefit of using these hearing aids, there is a natural desire to continue their use because *everything* heard is so much clearer.

Reflective Questions

What resonates with you in this chapter?

What surprises you about this chapter?

What are you curious to learn more about?

Bonus Question

How is Listening for Clarity different from other listening techniques?

What was the difference in outcome between when you did and did not listen for clarity? Describe your state of mind in each case.

My Insights

CHAPTER THREE

Impact of Listening

T here is a common misunderstanding that the primary component of communication is speaking. Of far greater value, though, is the component of listening. One of the major complaints people express about poor communication has little to do with words. It has to do with not feeling heard. And feeling heard has nothing to do with the listener's ability to understand words.

High-quality listening is a state of mind uncluttered with opinion and judgment. There is a genuine desire to understand what the speaker is trying to convey.

Impact of Listening

Distracted Listener	Speaker's Experience
Preoccupied Evaluative Criticized Self-Absorbed	Disconnected; Disengaged Judged Wrong; Inadequate Distanced; Isolated

Impact of Listening (continued)

Engaged Listener	Speaker's Experience
Establishes Rapport Engaged Absorbed Asks Clarifying Questions	Respected; Listens Deeply Connected Valued Heard; Understood

Practical Benefits of Listening with a Clear Mind

When the listener has a clear mind, there is a better likelihood the speaker will settle down and become clear as well. The speaker will benefit from the experience and become an example of listening to others more effectively.

Listening in a clear mind is not only more effective, it is more practical and efficient. There is exploratory dialogue, a results-oriented focus, fewer mistakes are made, and less re-work is needed. There are fewer arguments, greater productivity, and increased customer and employee satisfaction.

There is a common misunderstanding that the primary component of communication is speaking.

Listening to others with a clear mind is a result of understanding the importance of listening to, and being guided by, your own innate wisdom.

Reflective Questions

What resonates with you in this chapter?

What surprises you about this chapter?

What are you curious to learn more about?

Bonus Question

What is your experience of being listened to by a distracted listener? Engaged Listener?

What is an example of when you were the distracted listener? Engaged listener?

My Insights

CHAPTER FOUR

Levels of Listening

For Understanding

- Of the Entire Message
    - Without the filter of opinion.
    - Not just the words spoken.
- Beyond the Words
    - Interest in more than just the message.
    - Understand how someone could think the way they do whether or not you think the same way.
    - Interested in the feeling and message underneath the words.
    - Focus is on learning without bias.

For Implication

- How the message affects broader issues in professional and personal life.
- Insights about life lessons.
- Relevant examples will occur to you and may be shared, if appropriate.

For Application

- How to use what is learned regarding a specific situation, issue, or setting.
- Practical application of broad message.
- Relevant examples will occur to you and may be shared, if appropriate.

To Agree

- Sort for portions of the message that are in agreement with your own.
- Practical application of broad message.
- Interest in sharing own views to keep testing for agreement and validation.
- Feelings range from relief to vindication.
- ***Deep listening has stopped***

To Disagree

- Sort for portions of the message with which you disagree.
- Strong desire to share own views for purpose of debate and to shoot holes in or destroy their message.
- You are an argument waiting to happen.
- Feelings of skepticism, suspicion, cynicism even before the other person has begun to speak.
- ***Deep listening has stopped***

To Tell My Story

- Listen only until a personal story comes to mind that you can tell.
- Horizontal conversations begin; one-upsmanship; "war" stories.
- Interrupts and derails the speaker.
- Irrelevant self-focus prevails.
- ***Deep listening has stopped***

Disengaged

- No listening is occurring.
- Relevant contribution will not be made.
- You are occupying space on a chair.

Reflective Questions

What resonates with you in this chapter?

What surprises you about this chapter?

What are you curious to learn more about?

Bonus Question

What levels of listening do you seem to visit more often? What is an example of when you've listened at a deeper level?

My Insights

CHAPTER FIVE

Thought Habits That Impair Listening

Compare	To our own view or that of others
Jump to Conclusions	Assume you already know what they think and feel; attempt to mind read
Interrupt	Insert own view; change the topic or course of discussion; disruptive to their flow of thought; what's on your mind is more important than what they have to say
Multitask	Assume you can listen and do other things at the same time; believe own activities are of greater importance than listening to them
Look for Motive	Assume there is an ulterior motive; hidden agenda; try to second-guess them

Rehearse	What you plan to say next; tolerate their words until you can get to your preconceived speech
Filter	Listen for selected information; avoid other information or views
Judge	Look for agreement with or find fault with what they say
Day Dream	Go off on mental tangents; stop listening to them
Identify	Relate what they say to own experience and draw conclusions pertinent to you
Give Advice	Try to solve their problems; expect them to solve their problems your way
Reframe	Put a spin on what they are saying; decide you know what they *really* mean
On Broadcast	Dominate the discussion; speak rather than listen
Self-Important	Condescending attempts to teach them your wisdom; pontificate; it's all about you

Self-Righteous	Try to convince them to agree with you; argue; put-down; don't want input, correction, different view; point out the error of their ways and how right you are; stubborn
Derail	Change the subject; get them off track; joke it off; get them off their game
Placate	Condescending agreement

We all have thought habits that impede our listening. Are some of these habits familiar to you? Which ones are more prevalent for you?

Reflective Questions

What resonates with you in this chapter?

What surprises you about this chapter?

What are you curious to learn more about?

Bonus Question

What are some typical thought habits for you? What has been the impact?

My Insights

CHAPTER SIX

Conversation, Discussion, Dialogue

How much of your life do you spend talking? How much of your life do you spend listening to others talk? Have you ever known someone who thinks talking is the only form of communication? Do you ever talk to yourself when you are alone? Do you ever answer?

From the time we are born, someone is talking to us. One of our big milestones in life is saying our first word. Parents ask other parents if the little bundle in blankets is talking yet. Some of us get concerned that others might be angry, disengaged, or depressed if they *aren't* talking.

What is this fascination with talking?

Like it or not, whether spoken word or sign language, talking is a major form of communication between people. It is especially important in the workplace because most business actions require verbal discourse. Talk is here to stay. What we often forget is there are different levels of talk; each with a different purpose and impact on outcome. The level used will make a tremendous difference in the result of the discourse.

There are three primary levels of talk; for ease of review, we'll call them Conversation, Discussion, and Dialogue.

Key Points—Conversation, Discussion, Dialogue

Conversation

- This is the most informal level and usually takes the form of light chat with friends or strangers.

- There is little expectation or desire that an outcome, result, or accomplishment will occur.

- Listening may be superficial or engrossed.

- There is no formal agenda and a variety of topics will be touched on in minimal or moderate depth.

- Topics may or may not reappear in subsequent conversations.

Discussion

- There is a greater sense of formality and discussion that usually occurs between people who know each other in a business setting where the organization is the source of connection.

- There is an expectation that all people will talk and there will be a result, outcome, or decision. Brainstorming for options and alternatives is common but often ends in frequent expression of the same opinions by the few.

- Listening is more often focused on differences and similarities between points of view, and alliances are commonly formed based on those views.

- An agenda or list of topics is common. Amount of time spent or vocal volume can be confused with depth of review and importance of the subject.

Key Points—Conversation, Discussion, Dialogue (continued)

Discussion (continued)

- Topics often are tabled and reappear in subsequent discussions, or decisions are made that are not uniformly understood or supported.

Dialogue

- A clear state of mind is the necessary foundational ingredient. The atmosphere is collegial and is not contingent upon whether people know each other.

- There is an expectation that the first task is to clarify the purpose and common ground for the dialogue. The purpose is the collective overarching reason the relationship or organization exists. The goal is to reach a decision in alignment with the purpose.

- Listening with a clear and open mind is a priority. More than a *willingness* to hear from each person, there is a *desire* to hear and learn from each participant. Opinions and alternatives are explored, and thoughtful consideration is given to individual and collective ideas. Ideas build on each other and become something completely new.

- An agenda or list of topics may be used most effectively as a point to launch dialogue. There is flexibility to move to other topics if they are paramount to the overall theme.

Key Points—Conversation, Discussion, Dialogue (continued)

Dialogue (continued)

- Alignment is the desired result whether or not there is total agreement with each element of the approach. There is generally no sense of individual ownership of the decision made. The decision is owned and supported by the group as a whole privately and publicly. Topics are revisited when necessary to improve upon the previous decision.

We all engage in each of these levels of communication and there is nothing good/bad, right/wrong with the first two levels. They are perfectly normal, and they are not linear or sequential. We just need to be aware of what we are trying to accomplish so that whatever mode of talking we choose satisfies an underlying need.

The difference between these levels has nothing to do with the names we've used. They are differentiated by tone, spirit, and state of mind. The tone of dialogue is collegial and respectful, the spirit is broadly inclusive and mindful of purpose, and the state of mind is open, clear, and curious.

Dialogue is an egoless process. Self-image is not as important as the overall best interests of the group, organization, or relationship. Results derived from dialogue are clearer, more uniformly understood and supported, and have greater leverage and sustainability.

The kind of talking that occurs in a state of dialogue is more than words floating in the air. It's a way to communicate at a level that enriches what we do and who we are.

Reflective Questions

What resonates with you in this chapter?

What surprises you about this chapter?

What are you curious to learn more about?

Bonus Question

Which types of discourse are more common in your business meetings? How could you contribute to a change?

My Insights

CHAPTER SEVEN

The Art of Dialogue

Imagine you're in a meeting with serious business on the agenda, and the atmosphere is one of interest, curiosity, and respect. Even complex decisions seem almost effortless. Okay, same kind of meeting, same serious agenda, but there's a definite difference in the tone. This one is permeated with poor listening and contentious competition for opinion-delivering air time.

For a lot of people, the first scenario seems like a fluke, and the second seems like the norm. What about you? Would you like to reverse the norm?

No matter what kind of business you're in, there is a constant need to be flexible and creative, to pivot on a dime, to anticipate and be responsive to constantly changing conditions. Any shift in personal, local, or global circumstances will *always* invoke change. What will *never* change is the need to flex, create, pivot, anticipate and respond.

So, how can we maintain our bearings and create the most optimum solutions for the changing environment? Well, we don't do it in a vacuum. We need to explore options and alternatives. We need to listen to ideas beyond our own. We need to challenge the assumptions of others and our own. We need to make predictions about the future using lessons from the past and without losing sight of the present. We need to dream about what's possible.

The key is we need to do all these things collaboratively using our best collective wisdom to fuel the decisions we make and the actions we take.

When our natural collective wisdom is doing the talking, it's called Dialogue.

Our first meeting scenario was not a fluke. Dialogue is what made it work. Engaged in dialogue we enter a different realm, a realm of what is best for all rather than self-serving solutions.

Engaged in dialogue we enter a different realm, a realm of what is best for all rather than self-serving solutions.

How will you know if you're in a state of dialogue? There aren't any steps that will lead you to dialogue, but there are some characteristics that will help you recognize when you are, or have been, engaged in dialogue.

Characteristics of Dialogue

- An open, clear state of mind.
- A search for and discovery of shared purpose, vision, and common understanding.
- Ability to listen beyond the words being used to hear clarity of intent and meaning.

- Curiosity about, and respect for, other's views.
- Interest in others' ideas without being judgmental.
- A desire, more than just a willingness, to hear others' thoughts, ideas, and views, as well as the thought process in coming to that view.

- A desire to explore a variety of alternatives and options and consider possible results and consequences.
- Can support a decision without feeling a need to agree with each element.
- All participants are willing to share their own thoughts and ideas without being invested in or attached to them.

- Dialogue is seen as a way of learning as much as a way of talking about or approaching problems or decisions.
- A healthy, respectful, open tone in the meeting is as important as the content.

Having everyone at the same level of openness throughout a meeting may not happen all the time, but once you understand the feeling and effectiveness of dialogue, it becomes a priority to maintain. People are committed to helping each other get back on track. Sometimes it's as simple as taking a break to clear the cobwebs.

Dialogue takes the idea of brainstorming to an entirely new dimension.

It's not about one-upping each other with cleverness, or a rapid-fire cobbling of a series of views. Instead, the views bake into a new mold.

Dialogue is more than an exchange of ideas and opinions which remain laying on the table in no particular order. Engaged in dialogue, we have the perspective to see and synthesize the ideas into a complete system.

Dialogue gives us the potential to transcend individual ideas and opinions transforming them into something entirely new. And that something new enables us to flex, create, pivot, anticipate, and respond in a way that previously seemed impossible to imagine.

Once you have the hang of it, dialogue becomes the energy producing norm, and contention becomes the energy draining fluke.

Reflective Questions

What resonates with you in this chapter?

What surprises you about this chapter?

What are you curious to learn more about?

Bonus Question

How could understanding and engaging in dialogue more often benefit you professionally/personally?

My Insights

PART THREE

Practical Application and Evidence of a Clear Mind

Developing the Leader

CHAPTER ONE

Health of the Leader

If you've ever been on an airplane, you'll remember the advice to put your own oxygen mask on first before helping anyone else. If you are unconscious, it's difficult to be helpful to others.

Never been on an airplane? How about visiting a doctor? It's hard to take someone seriously who is lecturing you on the dangers of smoking as you sniff the aroma of tobacco on her breath.

Who wants an unconscious, unfit leader?

These analogies translate into good advice for leaders. You need to keep your own bearings to be able to help others maintain theirs. Who wants an unconscious, unfit leader?

Senior leaders are expected to help the company create, regain, and maintain its organizational bearings *within* changing or turbulent conditions. Their employees are knowledgeable about their industry, but may experience difficulty being creative and responsive to constantly shifting conditions. Typically, they are fatigued and burned out from being fearful and hyper-reactive to uncertainty and change.

The last thing an organization needs is a burned out, reactive, fearful leadership team. The business is looking for clarity and perspective to settle the muddy waters of change. If leading is what you want to *do*, then healthy is what you need to *be*.

Key Points—Healthy Leaders

- Assess the clarity of their thinking before engaging in anything.
- Listen without judgment.
- Maintain hope and confidence that a wise way to proceed will become clear rather than become attached to a particular outcome.
- Experience the same twists and turns of life's circumstances as other people, but will recover equilibrium faster as depth of understanding increases.
- See hope where others may not, and point it out so others may see.
- See innate health in everyone—without exception.

Health is Magnetically Attractive and Contagious

- People feel naturally drawn to those who are calm and maintain their equilibrium in difficult times.
- The calm of one person has a contagious effect on others.
- People want to be around people who have clear minds because their own natural clarity is elicited.
- When mental clarity is present, the healthy leader speaks to the innate health in others knowing that as they calm down, they will be ready to have their own insights.

Key Points—Healthy Leaders (continued)

<u>Understanding and Developing Innate Capacities is a Priority</u>

- Healthy leaders understand they can be of little help to others if they are not healthy themselves.

- There is a desire for congruent living. Walking one's talk is easier, more authentic, less stressful, and a clearer "message" than all the words that can be preached.

- All events in life are considered lessons to be learned which will increase the depth of all innate capacities.

- The power of the clear mind is used as a mental compass to guide all areas of life.

Leadership is a privilege and an opportunity to be of service to the best interests of the company, its employees, it customers, and its shareholders. It would be disrespectful not to bring our healthiest, clearest minds to them. To do that, much like donning the oxygen mask, we must *first* discover—and keep developing—our *own* healthiest, clearest mind.

Reflective Questions

What resonates with you in this chapter?

What surprises you about this chapter?

What are you curious to learn more about?

Bonus Question

What characteristics of being a healthy leader apply to you? What might others say?

My Insights

CHAPTER TWO

The Wise Leader

W hat is it about leaders that is so fascinating? Throughout time, leaders, their styles, and accomplishments have been placed under the microscope and dissected to see what makes them tick. What accounts for the similarities and differences among certified "successful" leaders?

Is there a single element, or specific combination of elements, that some possess and others do not? If so, could it be isolated and taught—or better yet, injected—to make all leaders great?

It's the subject of dissertations, research studies, and conferences, and one of the largest segments of books and journals. Each tome promises an elixir of leadership secrets that, if consumed, will set the reader on the path of guaranteed success. So long as the recipe is followed faithfully.

The X Factor

Studies of great leaders invariably mention something that cannot be explained. It is invisible and can't be measured. Only its effects can be seen and experienced. This X Factor often seems counterintuitive. Why are some great leaders so humble? They don't seem to put pressure on people to achieve goals, and yet they may even surpass expectations. Is something strange going on behind the scenes?

The X Factor is a philosophical foundation and understanding that people do their best, most creative work, when their minds are clear. The X Factor is simple wisdom.

Wisdom is our innate capacity to operate in a clear state of mind devoid of the mental distractions of insecure thinking. Wisdom allows us to discern an approach to anything or anyone characterized by respect, connection, and in the best interests of all. Wisdom is not contingent upon age, gender, religion, or personal intellect.

There is nothing wrong with intelligence. But intellect will take us just so far. It is limited by the boundaries of what we already know. Wisdom will take us to places and possibilities we never dreamed existed. Wisdom takes us where expectations, boundaries, and barriers cannot impede our progress. While our intelligence has a tendency to create complexity, wisdom always yields simplicity.

> *Intellect will take us just so far. Wisdom will take us to places and possibilities we never dreamed existed.*

Qualities of Wise Leaders

State of Mind Focus

- Understands and respects the role state of mind plays in the quality of decisions, actions, and results.
- Knows how to determine when the mind is clear or distracted and acts accordingly.

Philosophy

- Has a philosophical foundation that guides actions and decisions.
- Lives in service to a purpose and vision in life larger than self and unattached to ideology.

Curious

- Insatiable curiosity about all of life.
- Understands curiosity is the only way to learn without judgment.
- Teaches how to question from curiosity rather than judge from skepticism.

Listen

- Listens with humility and curiosity to learn from diverse perspectives.
- Actively seeks other personal, professional, and cultural points of view to enrich and increase understanding, and to illuminate other approaches, possibilities, and courses of action.

Reflect

- Reflects to challenge own beliefs and has the humility to learn from the past and present of self and others.
- Reflects to gain insight.
- Understands insight, rather than proclamation or repetition, is the source of sustainable change.

Decide

- Gives depth of consideration to a variety of courses of action.
- Makes decisions even when they may be unpopular.
- Is decisive without the paralyzing fear of failure.

Courage

- Unafraid to step out on a limb, fail, and get back in the game.
- Sees failure as part of life and examines it for valuable lessons for the future.

Communicate

- Communicates to inform, inspire, and elicit hope.
- Delivers the truth and expectations regardless of how difficult business conditions may become. This is done out of respect for the need for clarity rather than to induce fear.
- Assumes honest communication will be respected and appreciated.

Develop

- Places a priority on the development of the workforce to provide a solid and versatile foundation for the organization.
- Places a priority on self-development to gain knowledge and deeper wisdom.

- The wise leader is open, honest, and unself-conscious about continuing personal and professional development. Athletes exercise, musicians tune their instruments, both make mistakes during performance of their jobs, and they do it in front of the audience.

Teach

- As a leader and a mentor, teaches employees to fish rather than create a climate of dependence by giving them fish.
- Considers the role of teaching to be a vehicle for development and to continue one's own learning.
- Approaches life with a student's state of mind.
- The example set by this leader is both the teacher and the lesson.

Balance

- Gives priority to developing all aspects of life—personal and professional.
- Understands balance is a natural by-product of a clear mind and cannot be provided by structures and systems.
- Is an example of someone who is calm in a crisis. Knows the difference between acting calm and being calm.

An Important Difference

A number of these characteristics will be found in all leaders. The *different* ingredient is the understanding of the role of state of mind. Any one of these characteristics will look, feel, and create behaviors and results that are entirely different in a distracted state of mind where self-image and a high need for control is of great importance.

Wisdom is in the eye of the beholder. I know of no leader who would claim to be wise. Leaders who are wise are ordinary people who encounter the same difficulties and insecurities as everyone else. They just understand, have faith in, and pay attention to, the inner voice of a clear state of mind to help them stabilize and get back on track. In the end, wisdom is simply common sense.

NOTE: Although this article is focused on leaders, it could just as easily be called The Wise Employee, or the Wise Person. All people possess innate wisdom, and each of the qualities described would be exhibited in the same way regardless of occupation or position.

Reflective Questions

What resonates with you in this chapter?

What surprises you about this chapter?

What are you curious to learn more about?

Bonus Question

How do the qualities of a wise leader apply to you? Which would you like to develop further?

My Insights

CHAPTER THREE

Practice, Practice, Practice

What You Teach

L eading from a clear mind is the bedrock for creating a healthy high performance culture. And that requires that what is taught is lived. If that is not a priority, it will be impossible to be of best service to the organization. It's called "walking the talk." Part of the leader's responsibility is to teach people about their natural wisdom and help them discover their best thinking. You can't tell someone to take a deep breath if you're gasping for air.

How Do We Practice What We Teach?

Make Time for Reflection

I'm not talking about a process of reflection, but a reflective state of mind. Part of our personal and professional development is to reflect on our current understanding of how state of mind works. Actively look at our own life for examples of when the quality of our thinking has been clear or distracted. Look at the world around you, other people, news stories, and see the principles of state of mind in action.

Ask yourselves and each other questions to explore your understanding. Maintain a curious, open mind and listen deeply wherever you are. The entire experience of life becomes richer, more instructive, and more enjoyable.

Reflective thinking produces new or deepens previous insights. By engaging in reflective thinking as a way of life, you are better able to hear both healthy and obstructive thought patterns in yourself and others. If you didn't, you couldn't help them discover their own wisdom and clarity.

Engage in Creative Nourishment

Getting out in the world, pursuing your interests, and spending time with others is important. It's one of the ways to avoid isolation and actually stimulate creativity. Have you ever gone out on errands and had bright ideas invade your mind? Have you ever been mowing the lawn and had the answer to a business problem become crystal clear?

The answer has nothing to do with errands or mowing. The *key* is your state of mind as you go out in the world. Your mind was not struggling with anything so your thinking cleared. If you have a favorite coffee shop and enjoy planning your business strategy there, by all means go. There is energy around that is stimulating. As long as your head is clear it will be useful. If you start to worry or try to force yourself to be creative, it will become a distraction. It's the state of mind, not the location that produces creative thought.

Leading from a clear mind requires that what is taught is lived. You can't tell someone to take a deep breath if you're gasping for air.

Rest—Even from What You Love Doing

That may sound counterintuitive, but just as the body needs sleep to refresh, the mind also needs rest. No matter how much you love your work, engage in things you enjoy that don't *appear* to have anything to do with work. I say "appear" because everything in life ultimately has something to do with everything else in life.

The Mind Needs Refreshment

Refreshment may be in the form of a nap, a walk, reading a book, staring into space, listening to music, building a worktable, playing with the kids, or yes, even mowing the lawn. Don't be concerned about losing creative brain cells. In fact, proper physical and mental rest *increases* innovative and creative output.

Have Fun

There is nothing more enjoyable than doing something you love filled with passion and purpose to provide meaning in life. Sharing that passion in service to others is the icing on the cake.

Reflective Questions

What resonates with you in this chapter?

What surprises you about this chapter?

What are you curious to learn more about?

Bonus Question

How well, and in what ways, do you practice what you teach? What might others say?

My Insights

CHAPTER FOUR

Discover and Develop Talent

W hat topic typically makes it to the top ten agenda items at CEO conferences? Finding and developing good people to become leaders. From lip service to cellular commitment, you will not find one leader who doesn't think finding and developing the best people, and specifically strong leadership potential, is a priority. You also won't find another topic more filled with angst.

The first focus in finding good people usually means determining which candidates have the requisite education, knowledge, skills, and experience. The second focus is determining who has the best leadership potential.

The Norm

If you look at recruitment language and eavesdrop on interviews, companies want people who are: smart; creative; ambitious; loyal; team players; willing to do what it takes for as long as it takes; unafraid to take down the competition; able to hold their people accountable, drive to behavior and results, and get rid of dead wood; keep costs at a minimum; meet goals at any cost; ready to run the promotion marathon; clever enough to keep their department in the winner's circle; and able to perform other duties as required.

As a leader, one of your principal duties will be to develop the leadership potential in your people—create a leadership brigade for the future. The company has a training department and leadership development programs. Send your people to them, but make sure their goals and numbers don't suffer. And then your boss says, "Welcome to the family. Oh, and be sure to maintain work-life balance. We don't want anyone to burn out."

But wait, there's more. Next stop? Visit Human Resources to sign your papers and pick up your suit of armor. Imagine your surprise when you realize each department has a different suit of armor. Let the games begin! Can't you just feel the adrenalin rush?

Finding people with great knowledge and skills is easy. Discovering and developing people with a talent for leadership is an art.

Fast forward six months. Your boss wants to have a heart-to-heart. It seems you don't play well with others. The word silo is mentioned. Some of your employees feel under the gun and disrespected. Some are trying to emulate you and are now having difficulty with their employees. All of your people are feeling the strain on both professional and personal lives. You are getting results, but at what cost? What tarnished your shining star?

Something needs to change or this conversation will continue over the years.

The struggle and stressful effort implied in the normal view of finding and developing leaders is based on the premise that development is actually a chore to be fit in when possible. It happens more by default than by design. It may actually detract from getting the job done.

Is there a better way?

Creating a Healthy Leadership Infrastructure

Whether you are a newly minted leader or one who has been seasoned by time and experience, it is never too early or too late to consider the purpose of discovering and developing talent from a different perspective. Finding people with great knowledge and skills is easy. Discovering and developing people with a talent for leadership is an art.

People, homes, cities, and countries need a solid infrastructure to grow, develop, and stay healthy. Solidity has depth and breadth. Organizations need a solid infrastructure as well, and it has nothing to do with buildings.

Elements of Leadership Infrastructure

Philosophical Foundation

- Creating a healthy high performance culture means understanding and teaching the relationship between state of mind, actions, decisions, and results. Teach people how to recognize when their mind is clear or distracted.

- Reflect on the qualities of the culture you want to create that are congruent with the organizational reputation you wish to represent.

- Identifying, discovering, and developing leadership talent is a priority. It is a necessity rather than a nicety.

- A healthy high performance organization is comprised of healthy high performing people. The quality of the seed determines the quality of the crop.

- Set a standard for development that will benefit the organization, not only the department.

- United diversity is valued. Beyond gender, age, and ethnicity, there is a thirst for and presence of a variety of views and experience.

- Inclusion, collaboration, and respect are the hallmarks of all relationships.

Recruit and Develop to Leadership Priorities

- Set priorities for the kind of people needed to maintain industry know-how, achieve results, and develop others.

- Consider if the candidate has an understanding and respect for the curiosity, creativity, decisiveness, and resilience of a clear mind.

- Recruit and develop to those priorities.

Look for Successors—Create Incumbents

- Build the future in the present while learning from the past. Identify and develop new leaders as part of the legacy of your tenure.

- In the name of united diversity, know who is underrepresented in the leadership arena. Look for and create opportunities for development.

- Be clear up front about the scope of responsibility and expectations.

- Give short-term assignments with appropriately increasing levels of delegation, authority, and accountability.

- Create opportunities for long-term growth. Actively look for projects that need to be done.

- Be a mentor. Give people high-profile responsibilities and stick with them through the process. At the right time, place them in the limelight. Let them learn inside the ring as well as outside the ring.

- Link to a mentor. Find assignments and projects inside or outside your department with a leader who will stick with them throughout the process.

- Create broad-spectrum opportunities to give an understanding of the entire business and how all functions relate to each other and the final goal.

- Find or create cross-departmental opportunities to exercise the muscles of fresh perspective.

Link Passion to Talent

- Don't let people wither and die on the vine. If they have a great ability or skill in an area of little interest to them, they will ultimately suffer. Give them broad exposure and responsibility, but keep in mind where they will thrive.

- Find out what people are passionate about. When passion and talent are linked, people are more resourceful, creative, productive, and balanced.

Keep the Funnel Full

- When discovering and developing talent is a priority, your mental radar screen is always on, and your eyes should always be open.

- Send out search teams and talent scouts *inside* the organization. People stay fresh and engaged when they know they are respected and see the possibility to develop.

- Send out search teams and talent scouts *outside* the organization. People from outside the company and the industry bring a fresh perspective. It's good to have a mix.

- Organizations have a responsibility to the community they serve and in which they operate. If needed talent is unavailable, recruit people willing to learn, develop them, and deploy them.

- Create a training program that develops skills that can be used throughout the business community. They may become your employees, vendors, customers, or simply be woven into the community economy. Seek and develop—two important parts of the employment equation. Think big and broad.

- You'll know you are successful when your Talent Inbox is overflowing with hot prospects.

Hold Accountable

A tolerance for underperformance is antithetical to a healthy high performing organization. Do the appropriate training and development, but do not sacrifice the well-being of the business to your inability to reassign or terminate.

Some people are better specialists than generalists. Know the difference. Someone may be very bright in a specialized area, but not adept at managing the broader scope. There is no problem unless the job itself entails such responsibility. If reassignment is an appropriate option, use it. If it isn't, don't do it. There is no benefit for employee or company by trying to force fit—in fact, it is detrimental.

If reassignment is not an option, and all appropriate training and development has occurred, termination should not be avoided. Again, avoidance is detrimental to all concerned.

Although some expect termination will be the result and may even resign, most people are not usually pleased to hear they are not performing to expectation. They may feel singled out, unappreciated, or wronged. They may hear every performance conversation as a criticism. However, it is your responsibility to maintain levels of performance congruent with expectation.

If termination is the decision, remember to pay attention to your state of mind during the entire process including the termination itself.

The Joy of the Harvest

I always told my employees I looked at the organization as a farm. I was the Chief Farmer responsible for the quality of the seeds planted, and creating soil conditions that were healthy and nourishing for growth and development. I also explained that soil is healthier when the crops are rotated from time to time. And not all crops are planted or ready for harvest at the same time.

Part of the nature of a respected farm is that other people want the crops for themselves. As crops are sold, more are planted. Ad infinitum. And the quality of the soil is the infrastructure of the farm.

The Quality of the Infrastructure

The fact is, all leaders create and invest in the culture of the organizational infrastructure. The only question is, are we creating healthy high performance from a clear mind, or are we sabotaging the health, resilience, productivity, and achievement of our people through the insecure thinking of a distracted mind.

One of a leader's greatest joys is to watch and be part of the success and development of others. Investing in the organizational infrastructure with open-minded clarity and alignment of purpose is a privilege as much as it is a priority.

An organization with the talent of operating from a clear state of mind unleashes unimaginable creativity and innovation. Solutions to unresolved problems become the norm. It yields quantum differences in results through collective contribution far beyond the limits of any individual effort. It creates an infrastructure that is not only solid, but sound and sustainable long after buildings disappear.

Reflective Questions

What resonates with you in this chapter?

What surprises you about this chapter?

What are you curious to learn more about?

Bonus Question

How active are you in creating development opportunities for sustaining organizational capabilities? In what ways?

My Insights

CHAPTER FIVE

Rapport and Coercion

Two Methods of Influencing People to Get Results

All organizations need to achieve results. How the leader goes about getting them is based on one of two assumptions: People have an innate desire to do a good job, or people are innately lazy and need to be prodded, pulled, and shoved to do a good job. We are always on one path or the other.

Everyone wants to be treated with respect. At the core of innate health, people have a sense of pride in their accomplishments and the part they play in achieving organizational goals and results.

The Path of Rapport

Rapport is not contingent on elements of common interest, or how well or how long you have known someone. Rapport is an unconditional state of mind rooted in respect, good will, and having the best interests of others at heart.

244   Power of a Clear Mind

The Approach

- Applies to all people and all relationships (colleagues, family, friends).
- Rapport means "coming from" a state of good will.
- There is a general understanding that our self-worth comes from within.
- People want to do a good job; they recognize your right as a leader to ask them to do a job.
- People are decent; we don't need to agree on everything in detail, but we are resolved to come to alignment and live with the decisions that are made.
- People want to make a contribution and take others into consideration before acting.
- There is a desire to support others and be supported.
- Lead toward results through clarity and alignment.
- Actual authority comes from respect; rapport is a vehicle for building respect.

The Results

- An understanding of how the other person sees the world is achieved and respected.
- Aligned decisions, which allow problems to be and remain solved.
- Clarity of expected outcome and increased quality of production.
- Due to good will, people find ways to eliminate obstacles to quality.

The Path of Coercion

- Coercion is based on the belief that people produce results in relation to external reward. Decreasing productivity or quality requires the leader to exert increasing amounts of control.

- Methods of coercion can be as minimal as reward programs or as major as oppression.

The Approach

- There is a general belief that our self-worth comes from external validation.

- Adversarial relationships are the norm; the ends justify the means.

- Power, authority, and position beget punishment and rewards.

- People are basically difficult and don't want to do what is asked of them; pressure needs to be applied to ensure results.

- Drive to results through pressure and punishment.

- Respect is owed to authority of position.

The Results

- Varying degrees of resistance, including annoyance, stubbornness, rebellion, and sabotage, because people don't like being ordered to do something.

- Varying degrees of compliance as a result of pressure, fear, and intimidation, including good-natured quid pro quo, avoid punishment, grudging, "to the letter" compliance.

- The greater the authoritarian or repressive tactics, the greater the resistance and the deeper underground it will go.

The Surprise

Methods of rapport and coercion are not only inflicted on others. We inflict them on ourselves by playing mental games. We set goals and attach rewards for their accomplishment, or punishment in some form of deprivation if they are not. The problem is, we forget *we* are the ones setting the goals and the conditions!

Rapport is about respect. There is an understanding that self-worth comes from within. Coercion requires external pressure. Self-worth comes from external validation.

How often have you heard someone say, "I never ask of my people what I don't expect from myself."? Therein lies the rub. If we don't understand the basic assumptions at the source of rapport and coercion, we are likely to burn ourselves out while lighting the fire under others.

The Good News

We all get off track from time to time. We get caught up in fearful thinking. When our mind clears, we realize that as the level of importance increases, the level of pressure needs to decrease. For everyone.

The moment we remember our innate health, the most important realization returns. It is never too late to get back on the path of rapport.

THE CONTINUUM OF INFLUENCE

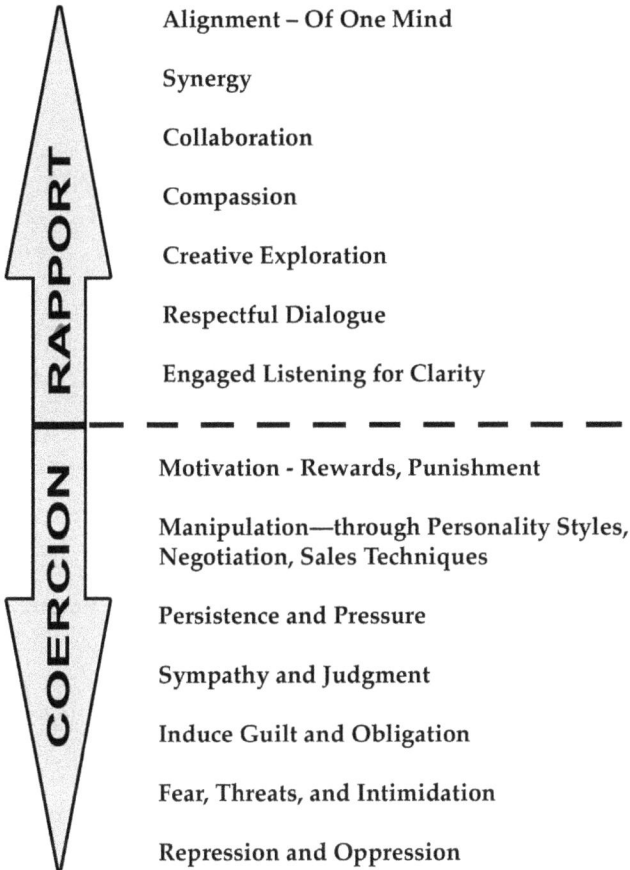

RAPPORT

Alignment – Of One Mind

Synergy

Collaboration

Compassion

Creative Exploration

Respectful Dialogue

Engaged Listening for Clarity

- - - - - - - - - - -

COERCION

Motivation - Rewards, Punishment

Manipulation—through Personality Styles, Negotiation, Sales Techniques

Persistence and Pressure

Sympathy and Judgment

Induce Guilt and Obligation

Fear, Threats, and Intimidation

Repression and Oppression

Reflective Questions

What resonates with you in this chapter?

What surprises you about this chapter?

What are you curious to learn more about?

Bonus Question

How do you see elements of rapport and coercion operating in the organization? What are your tendencies?

My Insights

CHAPTER SIX

Engagement and Attachment

Have you ever had a strong opinion about the way things should be done? No. Neither have I. However, I'll bet you know some people who do.

A Tale of Two Meetings

Attached

Some meetings are filled with individuals who are like a dog with a bone. They have ideas, opinions, approaches, solutions, and decisions in mind. They will push, pull, and prod to get their way. And, like the dog with the bone, they won't let go. Voices are raised and hours are spent competing for air time.

In business, this is called "robust discussion." It's not anger we hear leaking into the hallway—it's passion. If you didn't tussle and tug, it would seem like you didn't care. If you don't advocate for your position, who will?

If you don't advocate, if you aren't passionate, robust, strong-willed, or if you let go, you may be perceived as someone who is weak and doesn't care enough about the decision. You may slip down a rung of power and influence. And everyone is keeping score.

Result

The end of the meeting is never satisfying. Some people will always feel marginalized, left out, sandbagged, or disrespected. Egos get bruised, hard feelings have to be overcome, and critical eyes will be waiting for signs of failure in the final decision. The meaning of "engaged" to people in this group is to overpower rather than to understand. Hidden agendas are revealed. Support for and commitment to the decision will run the gamut from being happy to have won, to grudging compliance, to donning the robes of a good soldier. Winners and losers are declared.

Engaged

Meetings are conducted with a foundation of respect for and knowledge that each person will have a view and all views are necessary. Individuals are able to present their views knowing they will be heard. Questions will be asked to clarify and to understand rather than to become fodder for criticism. Passion is related to connection, vision, and purpose. People see merits and flaws in any approach—theirs included—without being judgmental. There is no need to impress others. Experience is valued but not limiting in options reviewed. Positions and titles are invisible.

As points of common ground are clarified, decisions evolve, personal preferences are set aside, and alignment is achieved.

Result

The meeting is streamlined, there is a sense of camaraderie, and no winners and losers are declared because it was never a contest. Relationships remain intact and, in fact, continue to deepen. People are supportive of and committed to the decision, approach, and method of communication and implementation.

Characteristics of Engagement and Attachment

Engagement and attachment are two ends of a continuum.

Engagement

- Priority is given to the quality of thinking producing the dialogue and the decision.
- Participation is predicated on the desire to explore possibilities to achieve the wisest decision regardless of who proposed the idea.
- The assumption is that alignment will be the outcome.

Attachment

- The volatility of debate is based on the amount of attachment to a particular outcome.
- Emphasis is on ownership of the idea that "wins."
- The assumption is that each person needs to struggle and give up something to reach an agreement.

Bottom Line

The fact is, we can all see ourselves involved in both kinds of meetings. The personal question is, where do we most often sit on the continuum of engagement and attachment? After all, the quality of a meeting is our individual responsibility and cannot be abdicated to the designated leader. We are part of the equation of the results *and* the quality of thinking that produced the results.

The characteristics of engagement and attachment are not limited to business. We take our thinking with us wherever we go. The more attached we are to our own ideas, the more we find fault with other's views, and the opportunity and likelihood of learning are greatly diminished. Every relationship we have will be affected by the prevalence and degree of attachment in our thinking.

The characteristics of engagement are also omnipresent. Being engaged does not put us in danger of being a pushover. Nor does it mean we will change our approach to a decision. But our approach and decision will be better informed and more inclusive. Relationships, regardless of agreement on issues, will be more authentic and respectful.

It is within relationships that we conduct business, live with families, maintain friendships, serve our communities, and participate in the commerce of life at all levels. What if we didn't have to waste time trying to figure out who we "really" were or what and how we "really" thought? What if we were authentically present and engaged in life without artifice—wherever we were? What impact would that have on the quality of relationships we create and the decisions we make? It's up to you.

Reflective Questions

What resonates with you in this chapter?

What surprises you about this chapter?

What are you curious to learn more about?

Bonus Question

What are your tendencies toward attachment? What is an example of a time when you distanced yourself from attachment and became engaged?

My Insights

CHAPTER SEVEN

Healthy Relationships

Healthy relationships are innate—a default setting. They do not require struggle and effort to establish or maintain. We are naturally designed to want to engage with others for personal and professional enjoyment and achievement.

To see evidence of the innate quality of relationships, watch children. They can immediately make friends. Time, effort, and common interests are not factors. Even when they get upset, they are resilient and the relationship as a whole does not suffer.

Adults teach young people how to make relationships complicated. Even as we grow older, the pattern of wariness and assumption of necessary struggle continues. Consider all the self-help and business material written about how to deal with different "types" of personalities, how to deal with "difficult" people, how to get along with a female leader, or how to enter the "old boys' network" without becoming one.

Granted, we all have different cultural backgrounds, but at the core, we all want to be respected. And the road to respect is paved with the ability to listen, and to value and forgive each other.

Key Relationship Factors

Listen

- Listen with fascination and wonder to understand how *others* see the world. Deep listening creates a stronger connection.

- Unconditional respect. There is no need to earn or meet requirements and expectations.

Value Unique Qualities

- Appreciate and value our differences or diversity.

- We can see "separate realities" and are not bothered by them.

- If we don't see the value, it results in conflict, contention, disagreement, dissension, and misalignment.

- If we do see the value, it results in respect, enjoyment, and alignment.

Forgive and Heal Wounds

- Have the humility to apologize and the grace to accept an apology.

- Understand that we all make mistakes and give someone the benefit of the doubt as much as you would like to receive it.

- Eliminate grudges and grievances—they haunt a healthy relationship.

- Forgive yourself first. You can't be present for a relationship if you are sidetracked by guilt, fear, or self-recrimination.

- We forgive others because there is a desire to reconnect and return to harmony.
- When in doubt, re-establish rapport.

The Health of the Relationship is a Priority

All relationships hit road bumps along the way. It is perfectly normal. When upset with someone, it's best to walk away for a while, and then come back when in a better state of mind. The popular advice is to "work it out" at the time of conflict. This can only result in lowering the spirits of both parties, and decisions will not be of high quality.

Healthy relationships are a safe haven. They won't fall apart at the seams just because disagreements occur.

There is a common myth that people in healthy relationships never disagree. Not the case. However, when all parties are committed to the relationship and the health of it, they recognize that the relationship has a life and importance of its own that takes precedence over the individual needs of the people involved.

A healthy relationship is a safe haven. Whether between two people or within a group, the relationship will not fall apart at the seams just because disagreements occur. When there are differences of opinion, they can be discussed openly and resolved. Things are not taken personally and none of the parties is invested in getting his way or having to be right. Instead, the focus is on the care and nurturing of the relationship so it will continue to grow, become stronger and more resilient, and remain safe.

Reflective Questions

What resonates with you in this chapter?

What surprises you about this chapter?

What are you curious to learn more about?

Bonus Question

What is an example of one of your healthy relationships? Why?

Is there a relationship you would like to repair or increase the level of rapport?

My Insights

CHAPTER EIGHT

Change of Heart

For a Fresh Start

Have you ever thought about a person in a particular way for a long time, and later found your view was very different? What accounted for the change? Was it the person? Was it you? Was it both? Which change mattered most?

A Chance Meeting

I recently had a chance meeting with a man I had worked with many years ago. Our relationship was not an easy one, and he was considered a very difficult person to be around. Harsh, judgmental, devious, and vicious were words frequently used to describe him.

We talked about what we had been doing in the intervening years, and it was clear from what he was saying his views hadn't changed much since we last saw each other. However, I noticed that I no longer had my suspicious antennae up, nor did I have a knot in my stomach.

It occurred to me that the world, and the people in it, must look like enemy territory to him. I noticed I was feeling more compassion for him than the judgment I had felt before. I listened differently and therefore heard more of what was concerning him, as well as what he was hoping for when he retired. He had dreams. In many ways, he was a different man—at least to me.

A Second Chance Meeting

I attended a meeting a few years ago and learned that a man I knew from a prior work experience was going to be speaking. I had never been impressed with him and I found it unpleasant being around him. I avoided him at the beginning of the meeting, though I saw he was trying to catch my eye.

During his presentation, I realized that my old thinking about him was intruding on my present experience of him. I wasn't listening to him; I was listening to my old opinions about him. When I realized that, I let those thoughts go and just listened. I found him to be knowledgeable, he was completely present with the audience, listened to their questions thoughtfully, and was able to speak to their needs in a relevant way.

We did speak after the meeting and spent some time catching up. He was gracious and talked about how he had been changing over the years. He was completely authentic. I enjoyed our conversation and we have maintained contact over the years. His wisdom has certainly grown and I was grateful we had reconnected.

A Change of Heart Requires a Change of Mind

The most important change was not in how the man in the second example had changed significantly and the other had not. In both cases, the most important change was the quality of my thinking *about* them. I had let go of my attachment to my opinions about them. I had gained perspective. I had a change of heart because I had a change of mind.

We cannot prepare for a change of heart. It may happen over time or spontaneously. And, like any insight, it will only happen in a clear mind. When we can no longer conceive of thinking in the old way, we have experienced a change of heart. And when a change of heart *does* occur, it provides an opportunity for a fresh start.

A fresh start occurs on two levels. It begins with you. A new relationship with your own thinking has been created. You are less attached to it. You know when to question current and previous assumptions, and judgment disappears.

You have a change of heart because you've had a change of mind.

The second level is that *every* relationship is open to review and transformation. Everything can be new again. Every relationship is eligible for a second chance. And there is no limit on the number of "second chances" available.

More good news. The door swings both ways. Not only can you give relationships a second chance, others can give you a second chance as well. Isn't it nice to know that a change of heart—a change of mind—a fresh start—is only a thought away!

Reflective Questions

What resonates with you in this chapter?

What surprises you about this chapter?

What are you curious to learn more about?

Bonus Question

What is an example of a change of heart you've had from a long-held opinion?

My Insights

CHAPTER NINE

Forgiveness

The Gift of Forgiveness

Forgiveness lets us cross the bridge to freedom.

Forgiveness is an insight that your own peace of mind is not controlled by people, or past or present circumstances. The insight is wrapped in feelings of humility, relief, gratitude, and compassion. Forgiveness is an understanding rather than a decision.

The greatest benefits of forgiveness are experienced by the person who does the forgiving. When people have forgiven, they talk of feeling lighter-hearted, like a burden has been lifted. The burdens removed are anger and ill-will.

Fear of Forgiveness

Everybody wants to receive it. Some are reluctant to give it. Why would a gift so treasured to receive be viewed as dangerous to give?

Because the traditional view of forgiveness is that it is something to be earned. And, in that moment, forgiveness becomes *contingent* upon meeting external requirements imposed by the potential forgiver. Judge and jury exist in one person's mind.

Have you ever done something that someone viewed as hurtful—even when that was not your intent? In most cases we don't *intend* to cause harm. But we do. And so do others. So, we engage in creating a mental hierarchy of harm with corresponding levels of forgiveness we are "willing" to bestow. We create yet another list of who is "worthy" of forgiveness. No wonder forgiveness becomes complicated!

The problem is that we become fearful that someone will take advantage of us. And fear is the parent of anger and judgment.

Forgiveness is the Short-Cut to Peace of Mind

There are countless stories of people who forgave terrible acts and frightening events because they *realized* their *own healing was at risk* if they didn't. They realized their capacity to forgive was their lifeline to move on and embrace life no matter what it included. When courts were involved, laws were executed and their peace of mind and healing was not contingent upon the outcome of the court's decision.

Forgive and Forget

"I'll forgive, but I won't forget." How many times have you heard that? Perhaps the voice you heard was yours? Here's the misunderstanding: Forgetting does not mean your memory bank has been erased. Our memory stores *everything* to be called up when needed as a source of review, reflection, and learning.

To forget really means to let go. Let go of what? Harmful thoughts. To the extent we harbor thoughts of ill-will or revenge, we will not have peace of mind. Gripping painful thoughts is like gripping the blade of a knife. The only person being hurt is the person gripping the blade.

Does Forgiving Mean Condoning?

Forgiveness does not mean condoning what was done. When you forgive, you do not lose your common sense and intelligence. If action needs to be taken, you will take it. You just won't be fooled by greed. You won't confuse justice with vengeance. You won't mistake recompense with retribution. You won't be burdened by anger, fury, and righteous indignation. Not only do they not change the facts, they actually *impede* the healing process.

Forgiveness Begins at Home

The greatest difficulty and greatest reward is in forgiving ourselves. To forgive ourselves requires that we look inward to consider our role in what we find painful. Avoidance makes it easier to look outward for a villain. The search is fruitless because we can't rewind the tape of our experience.

Forgiveness is an understanding rather than a decision. Forgiveness lets us cross the bridge to freedom.

Forgiveness removes the need for the labels of shame, guilt, fault, and worry, which get in the way of seeing hope and possibility for moving on. Again, it has nothing to do with condoning actions or behaviors. If there is a need, you will still pay your part of the appropriate price for what you did or didn't do. But I guarantee you will feel cleansed after you have forgiven yourself.

I was speaking about this subject some years ago, and a woman in the audience came up to me after my speech. She was in tears but elated. She had been harboring feelings of guilt for years because her child had been born with a disability. She had been convinced there was something she could or should have done or not done. Now she was pregnant again. Burdened by these fears, she was afraid of the future over which she had no control.

During my speech she had an insight about how only she could forgive herself for any role she may or may not have played in her child's disability. Imagine the relief!

Difficulty seeing the possibility of forgiveness, or the unwillingness to forgive, hardens our hearts so that we cannot experience the full joy in living. It doesn't mean we won't feel sadness or remorse. We will. They are normal human feelings just as joy is a normal feeling. But they can be felt simultaneously *within* a state of forgiveness.

And remember, if we can't forgive ourselves, we will not have the perspective to forgive others.

Forgiving the Past

The past is not our enemy. It contains the wonders and the blunders of our lives. Have you ever tried *not* to remember something? How did that work out? Have you ever had thoughts of the past intrude and take you on a journey down memory lane? I have. Sometimes it's fun. Other times I make deep grooves in the earth dragging my heels.

The fact is our past is here to stay, so we may as well make good use of it.

What can I do *about* my past? Nothing. This is where forgiving begins. As Omar Khayyam so eloquently stated in his Rubiyat, "the moving finger writes; and having writ, moves on."

Learning from the Past

What can I do *with* my past? Everything. This is where learning begins.

The *past* actually *serves* us. It serves as:

- A reservoir of lessons to be learned.
- A reference point for the present.
  - o How have you already changed your assumptions, beliefs, biases, prejudices, thinking patterns, and point of view?
- A reflection source for the future.
  - o What experiences could you explore that might hold untapped lessons?
  - o What experiences do you have a willingness or desire to forgive related to yourself or others?

I know a man who had painful feelings about his father. When we first met, he was adamant he could not and would not forgive him. Several months later he said to me, "I'm not able to forgive him yet—but maybe I will later." I heard hope and recognition of the possibility of forgiveness in that statement.

What Do I Do to Forgive?

Many books have been written about the physical, mental, and psychological benefits of forgiveness. And there are many. They relate how forgiving makes blood pressure goes down, cardiovascular, immune, and neurological functions improve; and people feel less stressed and find ways to cope. What's not to like? I'd like to add, all these books are well-intended.

However, when you are directed to steps and techniques to apply, your focus is on the external. What happens if you apply the techniques but still can't forgive? Have you failed? Do you need a different book?

Rather than looking externally for something to "install" in yourself, look inside at the capacity of innate wisdom you already possess.

The Power of Forgiveness

A single thought of the *possibility* of forgiveness sets us on the path of healing. Imagine *one thought* as the first paving stone to repairing a relationship with yourself, your family, a friend, business partners, or your community. Imagine a single thought of forgiveness having the power to enable nations to begin to listen to each other.

> *Forgiveness is a strategic business advantage because partnerships are created when grudges are not nurtured and ill-will does not prevail.*

Listen to the wisdom of the millions of people who have experienced great loss and great trauma who discovered the power of forgiveness set them free to engage in living a life of joy, meaning, and purpose.

The power of forgiveness does not reside in a ritual to be performed. Its *power* is in a single thought in a clear state of mind.

Forgiveness—A Strategic Business Advantage

Healthy high performance organizations naturally pay attention to relationships with colleagues and customers. When grudges are not nurtured and ill-will does not prevail, creativity, innovation, alignment, community focus, and partnerships are created. Solutions are not only of better quality, they often transcend what was originally expected or even thought possible. That's the kind of organization other businesses and customers want to engage.

A Final Word

It is never too late to forgive. There is no timetable. Forgiveness is an internal state of mind. The people and circumstances you forgive may never know it. Circumstances are over and can't be erased. Some people may have moved or are no longer alive. Many people would have no idea they were *on* your "forgiveness list." Even more likely, they wouldn't know why they were on it in the first place.

Forgiveness should not feel like a burden or an assignment. So, if I was forced to give advice, this is it: Forgive what you can now. The rest you can forgive later.

Reflective Questions

What resonates with you in this chapter?

What surprises you about this chapter?

What are you curious to learn more about?

Bonus Question

What is an example of having forgiven yourself? When have you forgiven someone or something else? How did it benefit you?

My Insights

CHAPTER TEN

When Performance Meets Expectation

Organizations are only as strong and successful as the people in them. In addition to engaging in one's own development, a significant role for any leader is the development of people at all levels of the organization. All companies have certain requirements for education, knowledge, skill, and ability levels for all positions. In addition, there may be on-the-job training and internal or external development opportunities.

Sometimes, no matter how much training, coaching, and development mechanisms are used, the employee does not meet necessary expectations and a decision about his employment status needs to be addressed. It's territory nobody likes to travel, but it doesn't need to be difficult or prolonged.

Leaders operating from a clear mind believe in the innate ability of all people to perform well. The creation of a healthy high performance culture is a priority. The question then arises, how long can we wait for someone to perform to the level of expectation? If we believe in innate ability, does that mean we don't have expectations about learning curves and competency levels? What do I do if someone is not performing his job according to expectations,

The understanding of innate ability and the need for competence are not mutually exclusive issues.

I've coached him for a long period of time, but he still can't do the job?

The understanding of innate ability and the need for competency levels are not mutually exclusive issues.

Slope of Learning

Each position should have the expectations and basic competencies clearly stated. Assuming the person has the requisite skills but is not performing adequately within the stated time frame, a decision should be made about whether or not additional time can be spent on bringing the person up to speed.

Most companies have a "probationary" period. It is during this time that training and giving people increasing levels of responsibility occurs to determine their competency and whether they can generalize their learning across situations.

Given the expectations of a job, there should be a learning curve, or slope of learning, within a range that most employees can meet.

Threshold of Results

The threshold is the point in time at which you expect the person to be able to function at the prescribed level of competency. These expectations should be clear for objective results and subjective values and behaviors.

If the person has not reached the level of performance required, the decision needs to be made to either continue to train if that is appropriate, move to a more suitable position, or to terminate.

When Performance Problems Exist

Continual extensions result in frustration for everyone involved and create legal issues in some companies. To avoid making a decision or delaying until you have "had it up to here" is a disservice to the organization, the team, and the employee.

The important factor is that you make your decision from a wise and discerning clear state of mind rather than out of anger or frustration from a distracted state of mind.

Important and unpopular decisions must be made in business situations. What will differentiate them is the way in which they are decided and communicated. When coming from innate wisdom, they will be clear, straightforward, and handled respectfully. More options will be apparent and others will likely have a clear understanding of how you came to your decision regardless of the level of agreement.

When Termination is Necessary

When the decision is made to terminate the employee, maintaining a clear mind throughout the process is crucial. You have no control over the state of mind of the other person. Their quality of thinking will determine how they react to your decision. The decision shouldn't be a surprise if you have engaged in continual performance review.

Even if they seem reasonably secure during your conversation with them, they may later regress due to distracting thoughts they take seriously as a result of worry, fear, thoughts of diminished self-worth, or comments and reactions from others. Upon reflection, they may feel that another chance is deserved. A colleague may tell them they are being treated unfairly or should fight the decision.

You may need to talk with them again, but unless drastically new information is placed on the table, reiterating the decision respectfully is your responsibility.

Promotion and Demotion

The slope of learning and threshold of results also applies to promotion and demotion decisions when position responsibility and accountability have substantively changed over time or as a result of restructure or reorganization.

Operating from a clear mind will allow you to maintain adequate perspective for yourself and others in the course of making normal business decisions for the good of the organization and its employees.

When Performance Meets Expectation

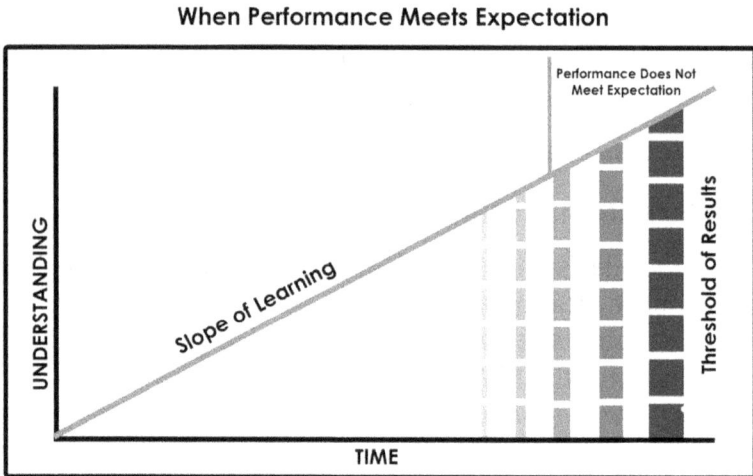

Reflective Questions

What resonates with you in this chapter?

What surprises you about this chapter?

What are you curious to learn more about?

Bonus Question

How would an understanding of When Performance Meets Expectation have been helpful to you in the past? Are there current situations which would benefit from this understanding?

My Insights

CHAPTER ELEVEN

Dealing with External Assessments

From Internal Health

What comes to mind when you think of performance reviews? I've known people who would rather have all their teeth pulled without benefit of anesthesia than receive or give a performance assessment.

I've known others who genuinely enjoy the process. They find it enlightening, developmental, and engaging.

In my experience, most people want to know how they are doing. They appreciate knowing if they are on track. They want to do a good job. It is certainly good business, and a fair and reasonable expectation, that performance will be reviewed.

So, what accounts for the difference between the two experiences?

Episodic Pro Forma Procedure

In many companies, the review process takes on the formality of a legal requirement. The purpose gets lost in the details of the procedure. The specifics of the forms and dealing with the procedure become ever more time-consuming and complex. Objective items are priority. Subjective items are tolerated.

The reviewer needs to "grade" on a curve or some other normative standard. The employee needs to polish his accomplishments so they sparkle like a diamond.

When all is said and done, nobody likes to feel judged.

Continual Developmental Process

A continual development approach is comprised of both a periodic performance assessment, and a professional development plan.

Performance Assessment

The purpose of assessments is to be of help to the leader and the employee as *one* aspect of a continuing development process. It is a snapshot in time of a larger picture. The review of performance should contain the objective elements of goals, standards, and expectations met, and the subjective elements of *how* they were met. This includes teamwork, collaboration, engagement of others, a big picture view, creativity and innovation, customer relations, leadership capabilities, and how they develop their own employees.

Professional Development

The professional development plan is more comprehensive and strategic. It certainly considers how the person performs in their current position. However, the primary focus is the strength, variety, and value of talents and capabilities over the long term.

How well do they pay attention to their contribution to the overall business purpose? Do they consider and anticipate the needs of the level(s) above them and the colleagues around them? Do they have perspective about business concerns beyond their own? Are they actively engaged in the development of their employees? Are they actively engaged in their own objective and subjective development? Do they tend to operate from an aligned state of mind? Do they value and represent personal and professional balance?

Key Ingredients

Humility and respect are key ingredients of any interaction. The leader needs to consider what the employee is looking for but fears the most. They want insight but fear being judged. Most leaders don't really want to be judges. They don't want to be viewed as enemies even when they make unpopular decisions. Both people have the opportunity to learn about each other and about themselves during the process of assessment and development.

Assessment and development should be an uplifting experience characterized by respect, possibility, hope, energy, vitality, and engagement.

The fact is, none of us has control over the other person's state of mind. Before engaging in a review, check your state of mind. If necessary, reschedule the meeting if you are unable to clear your mind—whether it is for five minutes or five days.

The quality of the review has everything to do with the quality of dialogue and nothing to do with time on the clock.

Continuing Dialogue

Assessment and development should be an uplifting experience characterized by respect, possibility, hope, energy, vitality, and engagement. There is no reason for it to be laden with fear and dread.

The difference is the state of mind from which the two components are viewed. In a distracted mind they are an obligatory drudgery. In a clear mind they are a privilege and an opportunity—for both leader and employee.

Reflective Questions

What resonates with you in this chapter?

What surprises you about this chapter?

What are you curious to learn more about?

Bonus Question

What are your tendencies when receiving assessments of yourself?

How might you develop the way in which you give assessments to others?

My Insights

The Leader as Coach

CHAPTER ONE

Coaching to Performance and Results

The Missing Element

There is no argument today that organizations understand they have a better chance of success when they have a set of values to guide their operations. The list of behaviors derived from those values is considered to be the best way to determine how the workforce is operating in relation to the values.

There is also no argument that organizations need performance expectations to guide and monitor how well results are achieved.

The Dilemma

The Jack Welch Leadership Coaching Model has been useful in identifying where coaching can be focused depending upon the area of performance that needs improvement or development. The key message is that business results related to goals must be aligned with expected behaviors and values. The *way* in which we do our work is as important as *what* we do.

What is not addressed, in this or any other popular model, is the philosophical foundation and state of mind from which the coaching is done. What exactly do the values and behaviors *mean*? According to *whom*? Ask any ten people what respect, collaboration, teamwork, drives to results, accountability, ethical, or communication means and you'll get ten answers—maybe more.

Likewise, performance to expectations is not as clear as it seems. It gets increasingly nebulous as you add scope, depth, and breadth of supervisory, managerial, or executive leadership accountability. The ability to perform a series of steps, produce a financial plan, or restructure an organization is only part of the issue. Can the person diagnose problems, create a variety of options, and assess possible impact for each from a system-wide perspective?

> *As invisible as it is, state of mind is the single most powerful determinant of how we learn, behave, coach, develop, and lead.*

The Answer

I have no problem with the merits of the Welch model per se. However, there is a crucial element missing—state of mind. The interpretation of values, behaviors, performance expectations, and what successful results look like is produced by a state of mind—in all cases. As invisible as it is, state of mind is the single most powerful determinant of how we learn, behave, coach, develop, and lead.

Welch Coaching Model

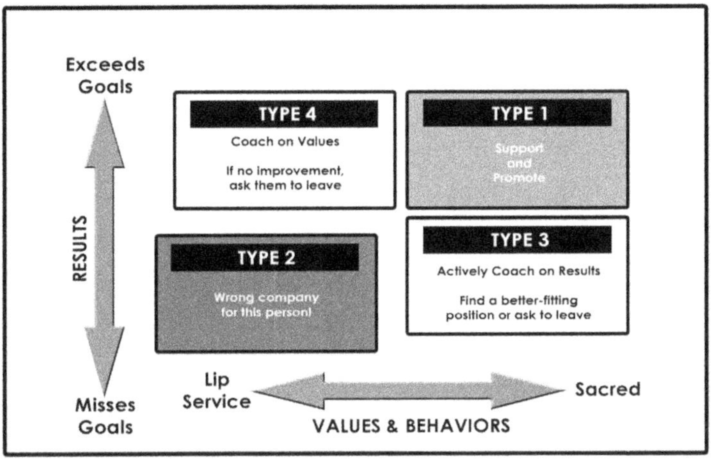
Exceeds Goals
RESULTS
Misses Goals
TYPE 4
Coach on Values
If no improvement, ask them to leave
TYPE 1
Support and Promote
TYPE 2
Wrong company for this person!
TYPE 3
Actively Coach on Results
Find a better-fitting position or ask to leave
Lip Service
Sacred
VALUES & BEHAVIORS

Reflective Questions

What resonates with you in this chapter?

What surprises you about this chapter?

What are you curious to learn more about?

Bonus Question

How would you describe the role of State of Mind in coaching to values and results?

My Insights

CHAPTER TWO

The Leadership
Coaching Model

From a Clear Mind

A Leader has many roles and one of them is being a coach. Development of people is one of the most significant ways to create a workforce that is competent, creative, productive, and resilient. Development is what produces a culture and mentality of sustainable and proactive change.

The function of development is not a program—it is an ongoing process that should be a high priority for any leader at any level. It cannot be delegated to another person or department. It can be augmented and enhanced by the involvement of other people, departments, or programs, but the accountability for a culture of development belongs to the leader. In this respect, the employee becomes the leader's client.

The Role of the Coach

What comes to mind when you hear the word "coach"? What do you think it takes to be a great coach? Maybe you've been exposed to a coaching model that taught you to memorize the six steps, nine techniques, and twelve mantras guaranteed to change your client's behavior and ensure your success.

Worn out yet?

Coaching is not something that is *done* to people. It is a process of development rather than repair. Helping others to develop and grow and gain clear thinking is not the product of *external* measures. Coaching is a process that allows your clients to discover the power of their *internal* resources.

When people discover their innate abilities, they realize they don't need someone else's steps and tools to develop or make changes. They understand they already have the equipment needed to gain and synthesize information and create their own approach as desired.

Development is not a program—it is an ongoing process that should be a high priority for any leader at any level.

As a coach, your job is to serve as a guide. And the good news is, there's nothing to memorize. Your coaching will be guided by *your own* innate wisdom.

CLEAR MIND COACHING MODEL

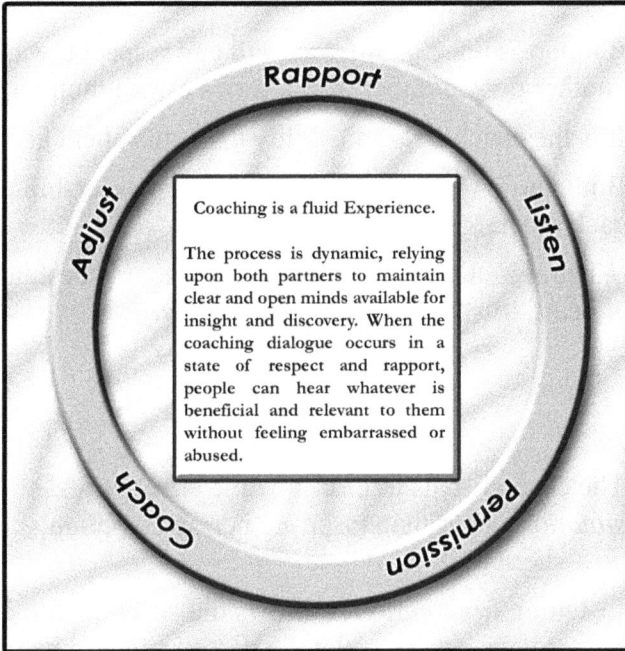

Rapport

Adjust

Listen

Coach

Permission

Coaching is a fluid Experience.

The process is dynamic, relying upon both partners to maintain clear and open minds available for insight and discovery. When the coaching dialogue occurs in a state of respect and rapport, people can hear whatever is beneficial and relevant to them without feeling embarrassed or abused.

Remember, coaching is a fluid, non-linear, non-sequential experience. These are not steps, these are elements.

Model Elements

Rapport

- Rapport is a feeling of goodwill and respect toward another person rather than a series of common interests.
- It is the coach's responsibility to set the client at ease.
- Both parties feel they are working in partnership with each other.
- When it is clear the coach has the person's best interests at heart, trust and openness will grow.

Listen

- The coach listens to hear how the *client sees the situation* rather than inserting her own opinion about how she sees it.
- Listening from curiosity allows the coach to ask reflective questions to let the person begin to hear his own thinking patterns.
- Questions may be asked to explore what would be useful and relevant for the client to learn about his understanding of the quality of his own thinking.

Permission

- Coaching cannot occur if the client does not give permission.
- If rapport has been established, and listening has been effective, there will be interest on the part of the client to enter dialogue about topics of business and personal relevance.

- The coach needs to test for permission frequently. The coach can tell if he has overstepped his bounds by the reaction of the client, who may be resistant to a particular subject, or feels like the edge of interest and understanding has been reached.
- The coach needs to understand the difference between lack of permission, disengagement, distraction, and reflection.

Coach

- This is the time when the coach can teach the client about his own innate capacities for a clear mind, perspective, and wisdom and help him understand the difference between an insight and a good idea.
- Coaching occurs in the form of dialogue and reflective listening.
- The coach continues to listen without preconceived opinions to remain responsive to the needs of the client.

Adjust

- The coach will need to adjust direction or topic depending on the needs of the client.
- Adjustments are also required when there has been a shift in the level of rapport or permission.

Key Points—Clear Mind Leadership Coaching

- Coaching is for the purpose of development, to help the client become self-sustaining rather than dependent on a coach.

- There is a fundamental difference between being dependent on a coach and valuing the perspective of a coach.

- A coaching relationship is not contingent upon how long the parties have known each other, or on expertise in the client's field.

- Most experts have coaches in the interest of continuing their growth.

- Behavioral based coaching is limited to that which can be seen or heard.

- Insight based coaching has no limitations and greater sustainability because it focuses on the quality of thinking that *produces* behaviors.

- There is an inherent understanding that each person possesses the innate capacity to have a clear mind which can produce constantly evolving insights.

Have you ever experienced a relationship with a trusted advisor? Have you ever been that advisor? Most of us have, and keeping that relationship in mind makes it clear what a privilege it is to be trusted and what a unique opportunity it is to be invited into a coaching partnership.

Reflective Questions

What resonates with you in this chapter?

What surprises you about this chapter?

What are you curious to learn more about?

Bonus Question

What elements of the coaching model would you like to develop further?

My Insights

CHAPTER THREE

Coaching is an Insight Job

O nce upon a time, coaching was looked upon as a grand experiment in changing how people behave. A wide range of methods were employed to find the best way to fix what people were perceived to be doing wrong. "Best" often meant most time and cost efficient. There was an assumption that efficient was the same as effective. The client was given a bouquet of advice, opinion, and directives. The prevailing wisdom was, "Just tell people what to do and how to do it and all will be well in the world!"

When an insight occurs, it is like a bright light shining on something you already knew but had temporarily forgotten. Insights are truly inside information just waiting to be exposed.

Lucky for us, the field has evolved since then. There is a greater understanding about the difference between being efficient and effective, and that people want to have a say in the learning methods best suited to them.

There are still two primary models of coaching—behavior based and insight based. Let's take a look at some characteristics of each model.

Characteristics of Two Coaching Models

Behavior Based	Insight Based
Behavioral repetition creates change.	Reflective thinking produces insights that create change.
Reinforcement techniques needed to maintain change.	Insights produce further insights that sustain change.
Expertise in subject matter.	Expertise in human thinking.
Compelled to give answers/advice.	Help client discover own innate capacities.
Focus on content of behavior.	Focus on quality of thinking.
Motivational methods employed.	Client inspiration discovered.
Listens to make meaning.	Listens to understand client meaning.
Has an agenda to teach.	Listens to teach what is relevant.
Focus on content and adjustment of client behavior.	Focus on quality of thinking that produces the behavior.

Insight-based coaching has benefits for coach and client because it is focused on the *source* of a client's behavior rather than the manifestations themselves. The source of ineffective behavioral habits is distracted thinking habits. As with any habit, once it is noticed it can be minimized and even stopped.

Behavioral coaching focuses on fighting the habit or replacing it with another, presumably less ineffective, habit.

Insight-based coaching produces greater leverage for deep, broad, sustainable change because it focuses on the rediscovery of the capacity for clear thinking. When a clear mind re-emerges, the habit naturally diminishes or disappears.

Key Points—Behavior-Based Coaching

<u>Focus on behavior:</u>

- Is endless, effortful, and exhausting for coach and client.

- It is impossible to predict all the conceivable behaviors to be exhibited.

- Client will not be able to control the impulses for the behavior without an understanding of what produces the impulse.

- Is an external focus on an internal issue.

- The client is ultimately at the mercy of outside circumstances to govern the experience of life.

Key Points—Insight-Based Coaching

<u>Focus on thinking</u>:

- Is efficient, effective and energizing because the quality of thinking permeates all behavior.

- Once the client understands thinking is the source of impulses, the impulses will begin to be more obvious and less compelling.

- Ineffective or unhealthy behavior patterns will be less tolerable and more easily dismissed.

- Clients are more responsive and less reactive to external conditions. There is an understanding that how we think about an event determines our reaction to it rather than the event causing our reaction.

- Focus is on the quality of our thinking rather than the content of our thoughts.

<u>Reflective thinking</u>:

- Thinking in a clear, open, curious state of mind rather than simply following a process or technique. The reflective mind is restful and therefore receptive to unlimited possibilities.

- Is essential for insights and learning to occur.

- Seems counterintuitive because answers and insights occur without focusing on them.

- Insights cannot be scheduled or forced.

- The clear mind is not an empty mind. Thoughts flow through like cars in the express lane.

Key Points—Insight-Based Coaching (continued)

Expertise:

- Expertise in how human thinking operates is essential for insight-based coaching.

- Coaches also have subject matter expertise in their own fields of experience, which may or may not be related to the industry of the client.

Listening:

- Is focused on the client's *quality* of thinking rather than *what* they are thinking.

- The coach doesn't listen *for* something specific, but rather remains curious about what *meaning* the client makes of his circumstances.

Wellness Model:

- The client is seen as innately healthy and complete.

- There is no attempt to "fix" the client because he isn't broken.

- The coach helps the client discover his own innate capacities and points out moments of health so the client can begin to have faith they will reappear because they are always present.

- Because the client already possesses innate capacities for clear thinking, there is nothing for the coach to install.

Insight-based coaching is easy, enjoyable, and respectful for client and coach. The only requirement for both parties to be most effective is a clear mind.

The innate capacity for insights is incredibly powerful. When an insight occurs, it is like a bright light shining on something you already knew but had temporarily forgotten. Insights are truly *inside information* just waiting to be exposed.

Reflective Questions

What resonates with you in this chapter?

What surprises you about this chapter?

What are you curious to learn more about?

Bonus Question

What aspects of Insight-Based Coaching would be helpful for you to develop more?

My Insights

CHAPTER FOUR

The Coaching Partnership

Yes, That's Right, Partnership

Have you ever felt like a lab rat? Or maybe a smear on a slide under a microscope? Not the nicest image, but sometimes it seems that coaches look at their clients as an epidemic in need of a cure. At some point we've all met, or been, that mad scientist.

There is a healthier scientific correlation to coaching that more accurately represents the clear mind coaching partnership. When scientists work together as colleagues, they explore the unknown together to learn what isn't yet understood. They share ideas and theories not just about obvious symptoms, but about the foundation that produced the symptoms.

> *When scientists work together as colleagues, they explore the unknown together to learn what isn't yet understood.*

That's the difference between traditional *coach-client relationships* and insight-based *coach-client partnerships*. In traditional coaching relationships the coach is the authority figure, the expert who examines the client's behaviors for symptoms of predictable problems and then prescribes the cure. Insight-based coaching partnerships occur in a climate of mutual discovery where each can learn from the other. Together they explore the *quality of thinking* that influences the client's behaviors. This leads to insights that guide the client to an understanding of the source of his innate health.

The coaching partnership, based on rapport, respect, and trust, inherently has great patience and latitude for experimentation and exploration.

People learn in their own ways at their own pace. The underlying assumption is that the client has the innate ability to clear his mind and have insights that will shift his experience of life without the need for coercive reinforcement techniques.

Key Points—Coaching Partnerships

- Coach and client work together as colleagues to discover what the client does not yet understand about the quality and impact of his own thinking.

- The coach is a trusted confidant, not a repairman. A confidant can provide another set of eyes and ears to offer the client a different perspective.

- Listening for clarity is a key ingredient in the partnership. The coach listens not just to the current views of the client, but to the quality of thinking that is producing those views.

- The client's quality of thinking is the *greatest leverage point for sustained change*. The quality of thinking, clear or distracted, *produces* behaviors and beliefs, and is therefore the focus of the coach's teaching.

- The client learns to explore his own thinking patterns. As his ability to observe himself increases, he will have insights that will *automatically and naturally* change what he does and how he thinks.

Key Points—Coaching Partnerships (continued)

- The coach shares examples and analogies as teaching methods when relevant to an area of development or exploration for the client. The client also begins to see examples of his learning in everyday life, which will solidify his learning.

- As clients become more familiar with their own thinking patterns, they become more self-sustaining and, because they have greater perspective, can actually begin coaching themselves on a regular basis. They enter into a coaching partnership with themselves.

Once you've experienced a healthy coaching partnership, two things will happen: You'll have an increased desire to continue and you'll seek additional partnerships. You'll want to be available to act as guide, teacher, and partner for others who seek the respectful ease of engaging with a scientific colleague without being subjected to the probing microscope of a mad scientist.

Reflective Questions

What resonates with you in this chapter?

What surprises you about this chapter?

What are you curious to learn more about?

Bonus Question

With whom would you like to engage in a coaching partnership? How would it benefit them? And you?

My Insights

CHAPTER FIVE

Contrasts in Coaching

There are two basic models of coaching: behavior-based and insight-based. The behavioral model is the more traditional approach and can be helpful. However, unless the thinking beneath the behavior changes, the coach and the client will always need to chase after unending permutations of behaviors.

The insight model takes behavior into account but focuses on the state of mind that produces the behavior. The client learns the source of his own behavior, and is able to sustain and make changes without being dependent upon someone else

Here are some characteristics you may find helpful.

Traditional Model	Insight Model
Tells	Listens; speaks when client is ready to hear
Behavioral focus	Thinking focus
People need fixing	People have innate ability
Gives answers	Asks questions to clarify
Teaches from predesigned agenda	Discovers possibilities
Advice, opinion, and judgment	Listens—then teaches what is relevant; non-judgmental
Coach feels compelled to speak	Engaged
Coach as the expert	Willing to learn from the client and deepen own understanding

Characteristics of a Coach

Traditional Model	Insight Model
The client needs to be "fixed"; judgmental	Sees the client has the innate ability to grow and develop. Has compassion and sees possibility
Do as I say, not as I do	Lives what is taught; pays attention to their own healthy functioning development
Focuses on the client as the problem	Focuses on client habits of thought that keep them from healthy functioning
Gives feedback even if it is too personal; too "close to home"	Gives feedback when client's mind is quiet and able to hear with perspective
Confident about what they know based on their experiences	Has confidence that being in a clear mind will help them make clear decisions and give meaningful input
Prepares an agenda	Prepares own mind to be patient and engaged

Characteristics of a Client

Traditional Model	**Insight Model**
Listens based on credible credentials	Listens quietly out of curiosity
Wants to learn how to change behaviors/skill-sets/tools/techniques	Wants to learn about their own thinking so changes occur to them naturally, are lasting, generalized, and sees relevant applications
Willing to put in effort; assumes learning is difficult and takes a long time	Wants to learn in a clear mind, effort is seen as worthwhile, assumes learning is enjoyable and not dependent on time or circumstances
Coaching is externally driven, generally received from a supervisor	Coaching is internally driven and available from a variety of sources
Wants to learn what motivates others and how to influence them	Wants to learn how to stay in rapport, have respectful interactions, and consider the thinking of others

Reflective Questions

What resonates with you in this chapter?

What surprises you about this chapter?

What are you curious to learn more about?

Bonus Question

What tendencies do you have in each of the models?

My Insights

CHAPTER SIX

The Clear Mind
Teaching Model

W hen you hear an analogy, metaphor, or example of how someone learned from an experience they had or heard about, does it ring a bell of recognition? Even if you haven't had the same exact experience, does it prompt you to think about how you have learned from your own experiences? Does it engage your imagination?

It doesn't matter *what* the analogy, metaphor, example, or lesson is. The value comes from knowing you have a capacity for *reflection* that *allows* you to learn from your experiences and those of others.

The capacity for reflection gives you needed distance from your own thoughts about an experience to see the possibility of a lesson and its relevance to the way you live.

Coaches have an opportunity to teach clients about their own capacity to reflect and learn valuable life lessons from *any* experience. As depth of understanding increases, insights about lessons will also deepen and expand.

The coach needs to engage in the same process of reflection and learning as they teach to others.

Why Should Leaders Teach?

There are many ways to teach, and most people think of leaders teaching by example. That's great, but not enough. When leaders share not only their decisions with their employees, but the thinking that helped them *make* the decision, it is more easily understood, and more readily accepted.

Teaching does not occur as the result of looking at a model on a piece of paper. Teaching occurs when there is dialogue about what the model means.

Being able to articulate the direct link between state of mind, quality of decisions/actions, and quality of results does two things: It helps others make the connection in their own minds, and makes it clear possibilities other than being reactionary actually exist. It helps the leader deepen foundational understanding, paves the way for further insights, and increases the likelihood that more decisions will be wise, timely, and of better quality.

Teaching helps you clarify and make the connection between what you are doing with how you are thinking. If teaching does not occur, people are left to make, and believe in, their own assumptions. You wouldn't leave it up to people to make their own assumptions about your financial goals. Why would you choose to be less clear about the quality of thinking that created the goals?

Here are some helpful hints when considering how to teach a topic so relevance will be more accessible to the client.

Teaching Model

Explore Your Own Thinking About the Topic

- What does it mean to you?
    - What do you make of it?
    - How has it been useful/practical for you to know about it?
    - Have you had practical or profound insights about it?
    - Why is it important to you?
    - Why are you grateful for knowing about it?
- Think of an example of how this topic has appeared or is relevant in your personal life. What was the practical value?
- Think of an example of how this topic has appeared or been relevant in your business life. What was the practical value?
- Why would it be important for someone to know about this topic?
- How does it relate to the bottom line/getting results?
- What would you tell others about this topic?
- What would you ask others about this topic?
- How does it relate to other topics we have discussed?
- If you were to make three key points about this topic, what would they be?
- What analogy, metaphor, or example would be helpful and appropriate?

I encourage you to expand/reduce the model to fit your own needs. You don't need to share every thought you have about each question. Remember, the process of reflection is expansive. The process of articulation is focused.

Reflective Questions

What resonates with you in this chapter?

What surprises you about this chapter?

What are you curious to learn more about?

Bonus Question

How often do you consciously engage in teaching as a leader? How could you develop further?

My Insights

CHAPTER SEVEN

Is Anyone Home?

Have you ever been in a conversation and had the feeling the person you were talking with left the room but forgot to take their body with them?

We've all taken mental vacations from time to time but, when coaching a client, it's important to know if they've gone on a brief side trip or left the country for good.

The coach needs to understand how to assess the distance and estimated duration of the journey. It's a bit like being a detective. The clues are there, but you have to discover what they mean *to the client* rather than making *assumptions*.

For example, the client may keep looking away from your face. Are they looking at something outside the window, at the mud on your shoe, listening to a sound, or reflecting on something you said? Clues are only an *indication* that something has shifted, and it is the coach's job to discover *what* has shifted.

There are Two Key Ways to Determine What Has Occurred:

- Notice if you are still feeling a sense of rapport, respect, and goodwill. If not, an adjustment needs to be made in collaboration with the client.
- Ask the client. They will know their level of presence or distraction. Make necessary adjustments with the client.

Four Key Levels of Presence

The Coach Needs To Understand When The Client:

Becomes reflective: This is a good sign. It means the client has been able to quiet his mind enough to fully employ all innate capacities. He is ready for an insight, can see the broad picture, and is considering how the topic relates to him and how he lives. He is interested in questioning previous assumptions and is not beholden to prior opinion. Priorities become clearer as do strategies to implement them.

How do you know? He may have become quiet, may not have ready answers for questions, may appear deep in thought, may say he is pondering something, or may display increased curiosity and ask more questions. He may seem excited about insights he is having.

Four Key Levels of Presence (continued)

The Coach Needs To Understand When The Client:

Becomes briefly distracted: Usually this is short-term. The client sees, hears, or remembers something that takes his attention away for a short time.

How do you know?   You may be aware of the source of distraction or he will tell you. If you notice he has drifted, commenting on it will bring him back. He may notice and get back on track or apologize. It might be something of importance came to mind and he wants to shift direction in the dialogue. The coach can certainly question if it needs to be addressed now or just put on the list to be dealt with at a later time. Either way, rapport has not been lost and the coach stays connected with what is relevant for the client *in the moment.*

Four Key Levels of Presence (continued)

The Coach Needs To Understand When The Client:

Withdraws permission: The client may feel you have overstepped your bounds, entered into a topic that is too uncomfortable or too close to home, seems irrelevant, or he just may not be ready to consider the topic at this time.

How do you know? He may seem irritated, abrupt, preoccupied, or start asking questions about why you have broached the subject. It is usually easily cleared up. The coach can ask the client about his reaction. It may be he thinks the topic is relevant but would like to gather his thoughts about it before discussing. He may not see relevance at all. As the coach, you should explain why the topic was introduced and why you believe it is relevant. Again, you make adjustments and re-establish rapport before continuing in any direction.

Four Key Levels of Presence (continued)

The Coach Needs To Understand When The Client:

Is disengaged: This is the trickiest situation. Some clues are obvious and some are counterintuitive.

The obvious clues may be that the client is upset or says he doesn't want a coach or is only engaging in the process out of obligation.

Nobody should be forced to have a coach. If you or they have the option of ending the process, that option should be made available. However, first do further intake to see if there is anything the client may find useful to discuss.

Remember, if the client is angry or upset about being included in the process, he may well be fearful of the consequences whether or not he participates. He may have beliefs or experiences of coaching being a repair station on the way out the door rather than a process of development.

The counterintuitive clues may include a very animated personality, a claim of great interest in the process, a ready answer for every question, and repeated commitments to "work on" something.

How do you know? The feeling of rapport is superficial and interest and commitment appear inauthentic. Listening is for content rather than meaning. The coach may feel tolerated rather than appreciated. You will know insights have not occurred because behavior will not change in a sustained way.

In either scenario, the client is highly mentally distracted and will be unable to engage until he can quiet his mind enough to see relevance in learning about the source of his own well-being. The primary focus for the coach remains establishing rapport and creating a safe environment for the client.

What's A Coach to Do?

The clues at any of these levels may *look* the same but mean something very different. It is the coach's job to stay connected with the client by maintaining rapport and listening without anything in mind but the best interests of the client.

When in doubt, ask the client. He will know where he went and how soon he'll return.

Reflective Questions

What resonates with you in this chapter?

What surprises you about this chapter?

What are you curious to learn more about?

Bonus Question

How would it benefit you to become better able to distinguish between levels of engagement?

My Insights

CHAPTER EIGHT

Pitfalls and Blind Spots in Coaching

Pitfalls

Losing Rapport

- Do your intake well so you can see what will be relevant to your client and can reach an appropriate teaching agreement.

- Staying in rapport and coming from a feeling of good will is key to establishing and keeping the coaching relationship. Rapport is the vehicle for results.

- Notice if you become distracted by your personal thoughts, such as, how am I doing, are they finding value, what do I do with so much silence, I should be saying something smart. Rule of thumb: Talk less/listen more.

Teaching a Client Who Isn't Listening or Does Not Know How

- Spend time on helping them quiet down.

- Spend time teaching them how to prepare to listen, and how to listen. In particular, teach them about levels of listening, and being able to listen without needing to know an answer. Help them become interested in exploring their own assumptions about listening, thinking, etc.

- Do not continue without addressing their difficulty listening. Ask them how they are affected by what you are saying.

- This topic is foremost to be addressed in any coaching relationship because growth will be dependent upon learning to listen. You may spend most of your early sessions on just this topic. It may be the most beneficial learning they have that will affect all other learning and experience.

Teach from Good Ideas versus Foundational Understanding

- Reflect on what you are teaching so you can speak from what is obvious and makes sense to you. Your grounding will resonate for the client.

- If you speak about the topic only from what you heard others say, it will lack depth and relevance for the client. It will seem like a superficial good idea, but will not have personal meaning for them.

Getting Off Track

- Follow their thinking: The conversation becomes horizontal. There may be some problem-solving, but there won't be much depth. For each problem solved, a new one will arise and the client will not be making use of deeper insight to solve their own problems naturally.

- Follow your thinking: The conversation will again become horizontal and will lack depth. You may get entranced with your own ideas, lost in memory, or become tempted to practice your cleverness on them.

- To do's: As long as they keep asking "how to" they have not quieted their mind enough to gain insight. You may answer a few of their questions to help them get quiet, but don't stay on that path. When they get the understanding and have an insight, the answers to "what" and "how" will naturally occur to them.

Listening "For"

- Your own agenda/interpretation: You want to know how they interpret the meaning of events, what they make of their own thinking, not how you interpret things.

- An opening: Looking for an opportunity to persuade them to your view, or to display your clever expertise is a disservice to the client. When an appropriate example comes to mind, you will know if and when to share it so the client will understand its relevance.

Blind Spots

Expectations/Judgments

- Comparing with others or an idealized image of perfection, based on the past, takes you out of the moment.

- Expectations based on what you want to see may have little relevance for the client. Any pleasure or discontent becomes contingent on meeting your (external) desires.

- The moment you get entranced by your expectations/judgments of the client is the moment you have shifted the focus from what the client needs to what you want/think the client should have.

Myth of Control

- Greater learning and extraordinary results occur when you let yourself go and operate from the wisdom of the moment rather than making things happen.

Interpretation

- Interpreting their thinking is only what you make of what they are saying. You want to know what they make of their own thinking.

Identification

- This occurs when you become distracted by how you relate to or identify with what the client is saying.
- Takes you into your experience rather than you learning what they make of theirs.

Misuse of Personal Examples

- Avoid the tendency to tell war stories. Getting overly caught up in personal examples takes you into your own memory and it is easy to lose sight of the needs of the client and step into entertainment mode, or enter into commiseration. Only use personal examples to illustrate a point.

Overstaying Your Welcome

- Attend to your rapport and permission—they are not without limit.

- Remember, the one role you have is as their coach. You are not their confessor or lifetime shadow.

Not Attending to Your Own Growth

- The health of the helper matters—your ability to keep your bearings is a touchstone and point of hope for your client.

- You can only teach what you know. Reflect and conceptualize about what you are learning and how it shows up in your life. What you teach will remain fresh and relevant.

- Pay attention to your grounding—continue on your own path of deepening your understanding. Unless your grounding grows, you will have little to offer your client.

Sympathy/Commiseration

- These are not empowering and promote a feeling of victimization. Having genuine compassion, understanding, and seeing their level of thought recognition will give you the necessary perspective to be of healthy assistance.

Taking Things Personally

- What they say, or how they react, has nothing to do with you. It is simply an expression of their thinking at the time.

- Taking things personally means your ego is either being bruised or inflated. Both are external.

NOTE: While these are many of the most common pitfalls and blind spots that may occur, this is not an all-inclusive list. Pay attention to which of these are most common for you and be aware of any additional ones that tend to show up for you.

Reflective Questions

What resonates with you in this chapter?

What surprises you about this chapter?

What are you curious to learn more about?

Bonus Question

What are some common pitfalls and blind spots for you?

My Insights

Practical Integration

CHAPTER ONE

An Aligned State of Mind

Have you ever emerged from a process for problem-solving, decision-making, or conflict resolution and felt like you had been dragged through a swamp? It's a common experience. When the process tends to create more stress than the issue itself, it's no wonder some of us consider avoiding resolution altogether. But more often, we take a deep breath and jump in.

Ask yourself these questions. In which state of mind will I be best equipped to make the best decision? Why would I settle for anything less?

In fact, there is a way to solve, decide, and resolve any issue with less time, stress, and effort. You've experienced it many times, but you probably thought it had more to do with the alignment of the stars than anything else. And while the alignment of the stars couldn't hurt, it's the alignment of your state of mind that determines the difference in your experience.

There are three models for collectively coming to a decision or resolution on anything, which I will call adversarial, agreement, and alignment. They are as different as a swamp, a river, and a clear mountain stream. The following models describe the state of mind, skills, feelings, and results associated with each.

Alignment Models

Characteristics of Alignment	
State of Mind:	Clear, open, undistracted Desire to come to resolution that will be beneficial to all
Special Skill:	Curiosity/Listening for Clarity
Feeling:	Engaged/Inspired Humility
Energy:	Generated/Vital
Results:	Commitment to the "spirit" of the intent of the law Alignment/Consensus - Collective Win Respect

Alignment Models (continued)

Characteristics of Agreement
State of Mind: Distracted by thoughts of trying to persuade others to your desired outcome
Special Skill: Negotiation/Persuasion
Feeling: Pressured/Manipulated/Motivated Modesty
Energy: Consumed/Effortful
Results: Apparent cooperative compliance with the law Compromise/Conciliation - Win/Win Tolerance

Alignment Models (continued)

Characteristics of Adversarial	
State of Mind:	Distracted by thoughts of trying to control outcomes and people
Special Skill:	Debate/Rhetoric/Argument/Advocacy
Feeling:	Overpowered/Overwhelmed/Hopeless Arrogance
Energy:	Drained
Results:	Grudging compliance to the letter of the law Victory/Defeat - Win/Lose Fear

The process of alignment can *only* exist when minds are open, curious, and clear. What are the odds that all people in a meeting will be in a clear state of mind at all times? What if you are in a meeting and you are the only person who understands the Power of a Clear Mind?

A clear mind and the ability to think in an aligned way are not contingent on the state of mind or understanding of others. It makes it easier if they *do* understand, but it can't keep you from maintaining *your* bearings. Alignment is more than a result. It is a state of mind. Because it is natural, your clarity cannot be robbed from you.

A little helpful hint: If you need to consider something important, alone or with others, ask yourself two questions. In which state of mind will I be best equipped to make the most effective decision? Why would I settle for anything less?

One person's clear mind will help stabilize the rest of the group. In a crisis, what's the first thing you do? Try to keep yourself and others calm so you can *think clearly* about what to do. People *naturally* try to maintain their bearings. So, the next time you are trying to solve, decide, or resolve, stay out of the swamp and the river. Clear your mind and enter the stream.

Reflective Questions

What resonates with you in this chapter?

What surprises you about this chapter?

What are you curious to learn more about?

Bonus Question

What are your tendencies related to the three ways of collectively making a decision? In what areas would you like to develop further?

What are the tendencies of your team?

What are the tendencies of your organization?

My Insights

CHAPTER TWO

Aligned with Purpose

Decisions...Decisions...Decisions

Have you ever been in a meeting where everyone agreed on a decision, but something about it just didn't feel right? And you couldn't quite put your finger on why? Maybe it felt incomplete, or less courageous, or more restrictive than originally intended.

In some ways it didn't seem to represent who you thought you were as individuals or as a team. Chances are, if *you* don't feel well represented by your decisions, others won't either.

If the decision made is not aligned with purpose, the best to be expected is good-soldier compliance rather than ownership or support.

What's the missing link? The answer lies in the feeling of not being well represented.

Who represents us? We do. Our decisions and actions are our press agents. They display the picture of who we are. It's not that most decisions are unethical or illegal. They just are not as focused as they could be.

The decisions we make about how we live our lives and conduct our business represent who we believe we are and what we are here to do. Not just the daily tasks of living and working, but the bigger picture, the larger purpose we feel we are here to serve.

In business, organizations have a broad, encompassing reason to exist—a purpose. And it's *never* just to make money. When we make business decisions that directly connect strategy, goals, policies, and actions to that purpose, we call that being *aligned with purpose.*

How Do We know if a Decision is Aligned With Purpose?

It's pretty straightforward. Ask yourself this simple question.

Does the Decision About to be Made Directly Relate to and Affect the Overarching Purpose of the Business?

If the answer is yes:

Proceed with dialogue about the decision, its communication, implementation, and review. This step is essential in testing the alignment of the participants in the decision-making process.

It is not necessary that each person agrees with each element of the approach, only that the overall approach is aligned with and represents the spirit of the purpose in its implementation.

This guarantees clear and uniform understanding of intent.

If the answer is no:

Proceed with dialogue about what the decision is meant to accomplish, and how it will support and affect the foundation and purpose of the business. If this step is bypassed, there will be argument about nonessential elements.

If the decision made is not in alignment with purpose, the best to be expected is good-soldier compliance rather than ownership and support.

Typically the decision is met with indifference. People charged with implementation will be less clear and more likely resistant.

Key Points—Decisions Made in Alignment with Purpose

- Are focused on central issues of importance.
- Save time by minimizing conversation about extraneous issues.
- Stimulate creative and innovative thinking about options and methods.
- Reinforce commitment to and support for the decision because it was made in a spirit of integrity and ethical collaboration.
- Ensure clearer communication and understanding of the decision, as well as why and how the decision was made.
- Result in faster and more comprehensive implementation of the decision.
- Guarantee more rigorous ongoing review and measurement of effectiveness because systems have been built in to the plan.

Key Points—Decisions Made Not in Alignment with Purpose

- Result in tangential or competitive discussions and debates about disconnected issues and personal preferences.
- Waste time either by irrelevant, unfocused discussions or by making premature decisions that are frequently tabled or re-visited.
- Sabotage creative energy and responsive thinking. Old ideas or solutions are rearranged with the hope something different will occur this time.
- Decisions feel hollow and don't resonate with the decision-making body. Camps result and those in agreement, or not, desire to keep their distance from the decision.
- Communication of decisions is in the form of a directive with procedural details rather than clarifying intent and purpose.
- Implementation takes longer due to resistance or lack of clarity and understanding.
- Review of effectiveness may be inconsistent or nonexistent.

Key Points—Common Misunderstandings

- Alignment with purpose has nothing to do with whether or not anyone *likes* the decision or the reason that prompted it to be made.

- Purpose should *always* be discussed before mechanism or approach to clarify focus and avoid confusion. A decision cannot be force-fit into purpose. The most effective approach is through the front door of the overarching foundation and purpose of the business. Once that is clear, everything else slips into place.

- A decision made does not mean it should never be revisited again. Conditions change and organizations need to be flexible and responsive to those changes. The purpose of ongoing review of effectiveness is to be able to intervene at the earliest possible moment when substantive changes must be made.

- Fine-tuning decisions on a regular, proactive basis is appropriate and beneficial. It exposes cracks in the system or highlights potential procedural improvements for efficiency and effectiveness.

Anyone making decisions, regardless of level in the organization, is a steward of the business purpose. When a direct connection can be made between business purpose and an action, goal, or strategy, the organization and the people who tend its well-being will feel fulfilled and well-represented by the decisions they make.

Conducting business in alignment with purpose will focus, clarify, simplify, and streamline *any* decision that needs to be made.

Reflective Questions

What resonates with you in this chapter?

What surprises you about this chapter?

What are you curious to learn more about?

Bonus Question

How often do the meetings you chair or attend gain clarity of purpose before proceeding? What is an example of a situation in which it would have been of benefit?

My Insights

CHAPTER THREE

The Power of Purpose

H ere's a question for you: When do you feel most alive? What are you doing or thinking about when you feel most fulfilled? What parts of your life best represent who you want to be? If time, money, responsibilities, talent, or any other barriers you perceive were not an issue, how would you be spending your time? What do you feel passionate about?

Clarity of purpose reduces mental clutter, simplifies decision making, and focuses amount and direction of energy.

Okay. It was five questions, but what came to mind for you? Sound like lofty questions? Well, they are because they point to the heights of human possibility. They step beyond fear and limitations of self-image. They peek in the windows of our dreams.

Most of us consider these kinds of questions throughout our lives. The good news is that while they invite us to explore the height, depth, and breadth of who we are, the answers are a source of *practical information* about how we live our lives. They *ignite our passions,* which *illuminate our purpose* and *energize our actions.*

Key Points—Characteristics of Purpose

Passionate

- There is a direct relationship to the amount and strength of passion we feel and how close we are to identifying our purpose.

- Feelings associated with passion of purpose are those of fulfillment, joy, energy, humility, and a connection with something outside ourselves.

- Time feels elastic and we can be absorbed without noticing fatigue, hunger, or pain.

- A sense that perceived limits and boundaries need not interfere with following our dreams.

- The clear, open, creative mind yields results that are often surprising to us and others.

Practical

- Options, alternatives, and opportunities are plentiful.

- Clarity of purpose reduces mental clutter, simplifies decision making, and focuses amount and direction of energy.

- Purpose provides direction for what to do and when and how to do it.

- Ethics become practical guideposts rather than constricting rules.

- It is easier to notice deviations from and misalignment with our purpose, making it faster and easier to get back on track.

Key Points—Characteristics of Purpose (continued)

<u>Pervasive</u>

- Purpose guides *all* aspects of our lives.
- No limitation on the ways and forms in which we can manifest our purpose.
- Evolves in scope and depth throughout life.
- An expansive service orientation goes beyond what is personally beneficial to what supports a greater good.
- Increased perspective helps us see the whole picture as well as the systems within to make more comprehensive adjustments in our actions to maintain alignment with our purpose.

Moving quickly in the wrong direction gives us the illusion of progress. A sense of purpose enhances efficiency and effectiveness in *all* aspects of our lives. We don't waste time and energy going off on unproductive side roads.

Every person and every business has a purpose for being. The nature of each purpose may be similar, but the manifestations of each will be unique. The power of purpose is that it acts as a simple litmus test for every decision we could possibly make in our lives.

The Paradox

How do we find our purpose? We don't. The harder we try to search for our purpose, the more elusive it will be. Purpose finds us. It is *discovered* by listening to our innate wisdom. And the best way to tune in to our wisdom is through the power of reflection.

Reflecting on questions such as those posed at the beginning of this article can be a short-cut to help us more clearly discern our purpose, identify our possible manifestations, and discover how *what we do* can be aligned with *who we are*.

Reflective Questions

What resonates with you in this chapter?

What surprises you about this chapter?

What are you curious to learn more about?

Bonus Question

How has your sense of personal purpose helped you make decisions? How has your understanding of business purpose helped you make decisions?

My Insights

CHAPTER FOUR

What's in a Team?

A team is two or more people who come together, by design or default, short or long term, to collectively engage in activities to achieve a common goal in service to a larger purpose.

In business, people are generally brought together by design. They didn't all accidentally show up at a company one day with nothing else to do. They applied or were recruited, and they joined for a reason. They made a decision to join a company and join a team because that is how business gets done. They may not have chosen the individuals, but there is an expectation that teams exist, each person is part of one, and they are to operate collaboratively.

There is an assumption that the members of the team have individual knowledge and skill beneficial to the goal and purpose of the business. It is also assumed that the collection and variety of individual knowledge and skill will provide synergy—the understanding that the whole is greater than the sum of its parts.

What Could Possibly Go Wrong?

There seems to be some magical thinking that if a group of people assemble, are given their terrain, responsibilities, the financial, technological, and human resources to do their jobs, and pledge allegiance to their leader, all will proceed without a hitch.

A honeymoon period often ensues when people get to know each other and are engaged in learning about and understanding the scope of the business and their role in it. The newcomer is open-minded and curious about the new environment, and wants to fit in and do a good job.

The Fear Factor

The most predictable source of disruption and unhappiness in the workplace is people. More specifically, "other" people. Just when you think you've got a game plan, someone becomes volatile, unpredictable, unreasonable, demanding, defensive, reclusive, or disengaged.

When people begin to feel they are not valued, treated like cogs in a wheel, are put in competition with or compared to others, or experience unrelenting pressure from above, their level of fear increases, and the level of mental clarity decreases. And when fear is fed, ego inflates or deflates. Trust, respect, listening to understand, collegial dialogue, attention to the work, and results start to topple. The territory looks hostile and they either attack or retreat.

When this happens to an individual, he becomes an outlier within the team. When it happens to the team itself, it begins to secede from the larger team. And the leader of the team will find himself at odds with the rest of the organization.

In either case, there is a desire to find protective cover.

Traditional Team Lore

There has long been a prevailing idea that teams take a long time to coalesce. They need crisis and difficulty to come together to be effective. Having a common enemy is more important than a common goal.

It may seem reasonable to want to defeat outside competition, but what if the competition, the common enemy, is another department in the same company? Seems like time to haul out the blueprints for building a silo.

Erecting Sacred Silos

What's mine is mine, and what's yours ought to be mine. That's the bottom line when silos are built, fortified, and protected by the infantry of defensiveness. Sound extreme?

Not really. The building of silos in business is an age-old craft—and for many, an art. People don't generally start out to build them, but when trust erodes, suspicion crawls out of the earth and starts laying bricks and mortar.

What may have started out as pride of function in the overall business purpose begins to create a bunker mentality that lobs verbal grenades at every opening. If you can keep others under fire, you may be able to distract your enemies from harming you. How did colleagues morph into enemies?

As easy as they are to identify, silos are not the problem. They are a symptom of a deeper systemic competition for respect and recognition. And they are as insidious as they are dangerous.

Teams becoming dysfunctional is a symptom of distracted states of mind prevailing. Unfortunately, there is a high tolerance in business for dysfunction simply *because* it is considered the norm.

What's a Leader to Do?

Teams are certainly comprised of people. And in business, by design or default, one of those people is the leader.

It is not uncommon that leaders and teams place priority and attention on the details of the decisions, strategy, goals, and tactics. A wise leader will be of greater service to the team and the business by placing priority and attention on the quality of the thinking *producing* the decisions, strategy, goals, and tactics.

A Crucial Understanding

Teams are not just a collection of individuals. They are not a collection of knowledge, skills, and abilities to be applied to tasks and goals.

Teams are a collection of separate realities. Teams are a collection of individual states of mind.

The Invisible Ingredient

The invisible, and yet most powerful, ingredient in a business is the quality of thinking of the people *conducting* the business. There is a direct link between the state of mind we are in, the decisions we make, the actions we take, and the results we achieve.

Wise leaders make it a priority to develop an understanding about their *own* habits of thinking—their own state of mind. They question their dearly beloved assumptions about what it means to be a good leader and what comprises a healthy high performing team.

Teams are a collection of separate realities. Teams are a collection of individual states of mind.

When they do, they see that it is perfectly natural for people to become reactionary and mistrustful when operating in a *distracted* state of mind.

They will *also* see that it is perfectly natural for people to operate with trust, respect, greater creativity, and make better decisions when operating in a *clear* state of mind.

The leader's role is to establish conditions that allow teams to operate at their highest level and wisest capacity. When operating from a clear mind, people see the business as a whole and complete entity rather than a group of disparate, competing departments. There is no need for pledges or loyalty oaths because the goals of the business are their own. They take pride in their contributions *and* the contributions of others.

Reflective Questions

What resonates with you in this chapter?

What surprises you about this chapter?

What are you curious to learn more about?

Bonus Question

What characteristics of the teams you lead or participate in could improve? How could you contribute to that development??

My Insights

CHAPTER FIVE

Signs of Trust Erosion

The major complaint and symptom of team dysfunction is lack of trust. It is always a sign that relationships are in trouble. Whenever a group of people come together by default or design, there is an ebb and flow of relationships that will include some elements of mistrust—especially if the group is together for a long time.

However, when individuals are committed to the health of the team and its broader relationship, these moments are transitory.

When people begin to listen more often to their insecure thinking, mistrust will increase. Of course, it's hard to find someone who claims to be untrustworthy. It's always pointing the finger of judgment at others. It may be insidious in its appearance, but left unattended it will strangle the team's ability to function.

Symptoms

There are numerous symptoms that trust is eroding at various levels. Here are a few examples.

Contingency: If you trust me, I'll try to trust you, as soon as you prove you are trustworthy. Being trustworthy may mean that you agree with me, or do things the way I expect them to be done, whether or not I've made the expectations clear.

Skepticism: Doubt, disbelief, disagreement, and a mindset of impossibility are in the foreground of any discourse.

Cynicism: Contempt and scorn are levied at the speaker. What you have to say is beneath my attention, nor are you worthy of my respect.

Suspicion: Active mistrust. I assume and create motive for your words and actions.

Shadow teams: If you can't do it, I will. I will set people or processes in motion to replicate what you are doing. I am noble because someone has to perform. I consider what I am doing to be "justifiable subversion."

Sabotage: Not only are you not to be trusted, I will actively hinder or cause your efforts to fail even at the expense of failure, poor quality, and increased cost to the organization. I will draw attention to your failure and do everything in my power to make you look bad in the eyes of others. A shadow team may be part of a sabotage strategy.

Results

Depending on the degree to which these symptoms are exhibited, it is essential they be addressed before they become embedded. In all cases, the other person, or team, is doomed before they begin and relationships become combustible. Subversive activities go underground, and though they may be done in secret, their results will eventually become apparent to everyone and usually at great cost.

There is a tremendous waste of time, effort, and all other resources. The CYA time alone is enormous. The amount of negativity required to sustain such actions poisons the well of respect and creativity.

Intervention and Repair

Without trust there is disengaged listening, unsatisfying communication, unhealthy conflict, poor accountability, unreliable performance, and lack of alignment—all of which indicate lack of respect.

Like it or not, trust cannot be installed in a team. Trust is a natural ingredient in a clear mind. It is up to each individual to let go of grudges and move on. If there is illegal activity, it needs to be discussed with the individual and reported to the leader. If poor performance of another member is impeding progress for you or others, discuss it with that person, or ultimately the leader.

The first appropriate action is to discuss problems with the individual involved—not others—not the leader—and never in the heat of anger. It may be helpful to get the perspective of a trusted advisor, but only to help you look at your thinking and to discuss possible approaches—never to create alliances.

As much as you want to be the recipient of the benefit of the doubt, others have the right to expect the same respect from you.

When teams attend to their trust level, individuals can look at their own actions and perhaps understand why someone else may have questioned what they did. Most people are not actively trying to be devious. As much as you want to be the recipient of the benefit of the doubt, others have the right to expect the same respect from you.

When Someone Cannot be Trusted

Although everyone is innately capable of trusting and being trustworthy, we have no control over when or whether someone will "see the light." Common sense indicates the issue needs to be addressed earlier rather than later.

After appropriate action, intervention, and dialogue has occurred, the question of membership on the team and involvement in the business must be asked. It is not a matter of who's in or out of favor. There is no room for sanctimony here. It is a matter of the health and effectiveness of the team and the business in which it operates.

How is it helpful to operate a business if there are people *unwilling* to trust in the first place or who *actually cannot* be trusted in the final analysis?

Bottom Line

Although the leader is ultimately accountable for attending to the trust and health of the team, each individual has accountability for what they *contribute* to the health of the team. If you expect to receive trust, you have to willingly give it, and make it a personal priority to nurture and maintain it.

The health of the team, and the well-being of the business, takes precedence over the ego of any individual.

Reflective Questions

What resonates with you in this chapter?

What surprises you about this chapter?

What are you curious to learn more about?

Bonus Question

What is your level of trust for others?
What is the level of trust for you?
What habits do you engage in when you begin to mistrust?

My Insights

CHAPTER SIX

Meetings are People Too

W hat is it about meetings that cause some people to say they would gladly sell their first-born or give their eyeteeth in exchange for never having to attend another one? On the other hand, some people say it's the best time to catch up on their sleep.

Admittedly, most of us have attended and probably even conducted some yawners in our time. Hopefully, we haven't had to sacrifice any progeny or body parts. But really, how did meetings get such a bad rap? After all, meetings are just two or more people talking together about a topic. Why is it that the very word "meeting" evokes an almost universal cringe? Apparently, not all meetings are created equal.

It's the ineffective meetings that can drive us around the bend because those are the ones most people talk about. Effective meetings probably should be placed on the endangered species list.

No matter how rare they seem to be, healthy, effective meetings *do* exist, and just in case it's been a while since you experienced one, here are some foundational elements to jog your memory.

Key Points—Foundation for Healthy Meetings

- Purpose and common ground is the central point from which all dialogue flows.

- High value is placed upon clear, open minds that have a desire to hear and understand others' views and perspectives.

- Frequency, time allocation, specificity of agenda, or how long people have known each other are not directly related to effectiveness.

- There is a greater amount of focused dialogue than unrelated conversational tangents.

- Alignment is the state of mind in which the meeting is conducted as well as the desired outcome.

- There is room and desire for exploration of views and information even if they seem to run counter to prevailing views.

- A high level of rapport exists regardless of how long the group has worked together.

- Listening for clarity and understanding is the norm.

- Respect for each other as individuals and as a group.

- Humility is the source of understanding that there is more knowledge and creativity available than any individual possesses.

- Courage to express views that may seem contrary, and to call attention to the effective and/or ineffective quality of meeting dynamics.

- Desire to discuss philosophical as well as strategic and tactical issues.

If ineffective meetings seem to be the norm, how can we have more healthy meetings? Who is responsible for the health of a meeting? Well, it's not the meeting's fault, so let's not malign them anymore, poor things. Meetings have feelings because *people* have feelings. Meetings are people too because they were *invented* by and are *made* of people. The feelings we experience in meetings tell us precisely the quality of the meeting's health.

Responsibility for whether a meeting is operating in a healthy way is ours individually and collectively.

Most people don't *intend* to have a lousy meeting. They jump into topics for discussion out of habit and under the illusion that speed will equate to effectiveness. Whether that speed is slow or fast will depend on preconceived notions and previous experience.

For example, not taking the time to discuss items in appropriate depth will result in those same topics reappearing on the agenda until they grow mold. How many times have you had that experience?

> *Responsibility for whether a meeting is operating in a healthy way is ours individually and collectively—not just the leader's.*

There is hope. We all have the inner resources to function in a healthy, progressive state of mind. Our frustration can be our greatest ally. It is an indication, an emotional clue, to the quality of our thinking. It lets us know *which* topics need in-depth dialogue and *which* topics are of little value, or off purpose. This is evidence of our innate capacity of perspective that allows us to see and set priorities. And like magic, old topics are settled and disappear.

So, is perspective the magic ingredient for healthy meetings? Yes...and no. Perspective is certainly essential. However, perspective and all the other foundational elements previously listed are byproducts of a clear mind.

The magic ingredient, and therefore the most important element in healthy meetings, is having a clear, open mind.

When that is present, rapport, undistracted listening, perspective, courage, philosophical alignment, and creative alternatives will automatically, and naturally, appear.

Reflective Questions

What resonates with you in this chapter?

What surprises you about this chapter?

What are you curious to learn more about?

Bonus Question

How would understanding the foundation for healthy meetings help you in the meetings you chair and those you attend?

My Insights

CHAPTER SEVEN

Healthy Meeting Dynamics

What's in Fashion and Vogue?

Have you noticed how fashionable it has become for people to complain about and show disdain for meetings? So much time is spent denigrating and avoiding them that meeting leadership has become poor and participation disrespectful.

Yet, the majority of business is conducted in meetings. Between two people or twenty, when people are gathered together in the name of business, it's a meeting. It's a place where proposals are advanced and decisions are made. It's a place for people to try out ideas, ask for support, and give updates on progress and achievement.

> *It may take two to tango, but it takes a team to make a meeting fail.*

It is also in vogue to differentiate meeting norms based on the rungs of the corporate ladder. Longer meetings are fine for lower rungs, but shorter meetings are proper for upper rungs. Some people say that members and guests of executive meetings need to think, speak, and act quickly. I'd be more impressed if they would think, speak, and act clearly and thoughtfully. Speed of mouth and volume of lung have nothing to do with intellect, wisdom, vision, or ethics.

The efficacy of a meeting has nothing to do with time spent or which rung of the ladder you happen to be occupying.

Meetings are a Microcosm of the Culture

You can attend any meeting and see what norms have been created and are tolerated in the organization. Those who say meetings are boring are often uninterested in anything other than "their part." Guests are treated as intruders and best interrogated and dispatched as soon as possible. Colleagues are tolerated. Some people read their e-mail, engage in side conversations, or work on reports.

When we are uninterested, we disengage. When we disengage, we are not listening.

When we are not listening, we cannot learn. Learn what? How we can be of assistance to another department, how they might be of assistance to ours, who might be a good sounding board, how the business actually works, the individual and collective roles and contributions to the entire entity.

It may take two to tango, but it takes a team to make a meeting fail. When we accept and engage in the norms described, we are complicit in the failure of meeting productivity and effectiveness.

Meetings are a necessity to conduct much of our business. Instead of complaining about what we don't like, let's take a look at what comprises a healthy meeting.

Healthy Meeting Essentials

Healthy meeting essentials are the responsibility and accountability of *each* person in the meeting.

Quality of Thinking

Clear Your Mind

- Check your own state of mind first.

- Throughout the meeting, ask yourself this question: What is the quality of thinking I am offering to the meeting?

Rapport is Sacred

- Establish rapport before agenda review. Nothing will kill creative productivity faster than loss of rapport. Rapport is rooted in respect.

- Monitor the level of rapport throughout the meeting. If it is declining, re-establish it before moving on. Clear signs of diminishing rapport include a decline in listening, an increase in the amount of opinion sputtering, greater attachment to specific ideas, and signs of fatigue. Check the tone of the meeting frequently to discern if it is lighthearted or effortful.

- The remedy is often as simple as commenting on what is being observed and experienced and taking a break. The key is *noticing* the decline in state of mind and making it a *priority* to re-establish rapport before continuing. Simply noticing makes the adjustment easier and faster.

Quality of Dialogue

Listen with Respect for Clarity and Understanding

- Listen for the message underneath the words. Don't assume you know what *they* mean. An assumption is usually based on a comparison to what *you* mean. When listening is filtered by agreement, disagreement, and judgment, nothing of value is learned and will not produce creative solutions.

- Ask questions to understand rather than to interrogate.

- If guests have been invited to present information, listen to what they have to say. Treat them with the same respect you would want to receive.

Let Alignment be Your Guide

- Use alignment ingredients as your foundation and guideline for dialogue.

- Determine important specifications for decision making, such as budget, timeline, urgency, importance, customer need/specifications/preference, etc. Dealing with specifications first streamlines the process of identifying common ground, and ultimately decision making.

- Discover common ground before looking for differences. It saves time lost in volleying opinions. When you have clarified common ground first, suggestions about possible approaches are more relevant. It is easier to determine whether your own suggestions are based on mild preference, strong opinion, or new information. Don't debate mild preference or unimportant differences.

- Dialogue provides a safe haven to test individual and collective thinking about a possibility or proposal. Ideas are more creative and responsive to need and less likely to become a horizontal detour of discussion or repetitive lobbying for personal preference.

- Stay on the relevant track. If someone wanders off point, help them get back on track, and allow others to help you return to the point.

- Remember, as much as you want to state your own point of view and have it respectfully heard, others will want to speak from their point of view and have it heard as well.

Quality of Decision

Test for Alignment

- When a decision has been made, check it against the specifications to see if each has been met or if other considerations need to be addressed.

- Look for alignment in principle rather than agreement on details.

- Determine if everyone supports the decision.

- Decide appropriate action items—who, what, when. How will the decision be communicated and by whom? How will you know if the decision is effective or needs to be re-visited?

Quality of the Meeting

- Debrief how you did as a team. Was rapport maintained and tone monitored? Was listening deep, engaged, and respectful? Did you stay on track? Did you operate within the spirit and guidelines of alignment? Where can you improve individually and collectively?

- Creating and maintaining a healthy, high-performance team means a priority is placed on reviewing progress along the way.

Types of Meetings

Each type of meeting is intended for a different purpose. More than one type of meeting may occur within a particular meeting time. It is important to know the difference when moving between them. The categories may appear on the agenda.

Information Only

- Determine if there is a more appropriate way to disseminate the information.

- If dialogue about the information is expected or necessary, a meeting is helpful.

Progress Updates

- Status of current projects, implementation of decisions, or changes anticipated.

- Possible requests for support or other needs.

Operational

- Approximately 50 percent to 60 percent of the items to be addressed relate to the running of the business.

Strategic

- Leadership and stewardship of the business.
- Corporate goals, achievement and performance status, and direction.

Philosophical

- Clear state of mind necessary.
- One of the most essential issues for senior leadership and often the most overlooked.
- Items relate to the purpose, vision, organizational culture, development of the business and its employees, impact of the business on the customer, shareholder, and community.
- Collective thinking needs to be explored.

Guidelines

- Meetings need a leader.
- The leader may decide to lead it alone, may have it facilitated, or may have a coach present.
- Rapport, listening, and ingredients of alignment are the foundation for success.
- Determine the need for an agenda. A list of discussion topics may be all that is necessary. Whether an agenda or list of topics is used, determine each item's priority.

Guidelines (continued)

- Determine the need for time slots. Time slots can be helpful for information or progress updates. They are not helpful for issues requiring dialogue.

- Maintain respect for reflection, insight, and dialogue rather than opinion and reaction.

- Determine who has authority and accountability for decisions made.

- End when finished. When meetings are conducted in a clear mind, it will be obvious when the meeting is finished—even if there is still time available on the schedule, or if more time is needed.

Setting Priorities

It may be helpful to look at priorities as you would a tree. The specifics of trunk, branch, and leaf issues will be different, but the categories are relevant from executive leadership to line staff. Regardless of their category, consider importance and urgency of the topic.

Trunk Issues

- Strategic impact.
- Corporate focus.
- Priority for senior leadership.
- Foundational issues such as purpose, vision, and culture.
- Nature and quality of key relationships within and outside the company.
- Developmental—business and people.

Branch Issues

- Tactical impact.
- Operational issues.
- Departmental focus.

Leaf Issues

- Activity impact.
- Process and procedure issues.
- Unit and individual contributor focus.

Decision-Making Options

Clarity of decision-making accountability is essential to avoid confusion and waste of time and resources.

- Leader makes the decision.
- Leader asks for input—then makes decision.
- Leader tables the decision and places it in the "parking lot" for a future meeting. Should be done primarily if additional information or expertise is needed to make an informal decision. Use this option with caution so the parking lot is not full of unmade decisions. If they are not important, get rid of them.

Decision-Making Options (continued)

- Leader delegates the decision to:
    - o   The team
    - o   A functional area
    - o   A specific person
    - o   A special committee for:
        - Information, research, fact-finding only.
        - Alternatives or recommendations.
        - Making the decision.

Reflective Questions

What resonates with you in this chapter?

What surprises you about this chapter?

What are you curious to learn more about?

Bonus Question

What healthy dynamics are currently present in the meetings you lead or attend? How can you contribute to the increase in their presence?

My Insights

CHAPTER EIGHT

The Aligned Team

All leaders and teams want to be aligned. It makes intuitive sense that people operating in alignment will get more done, with less stress and effort, and the results will be of better quality and more readily accepted by those who need to implement the decisions.

Alignment is a Priority

When the ingredients of an aligned state of mind are understood, creating alignment in any interaction becomes a priority rather than an afterthought.

Teams committed to alignment pay attention to the state of mind during meetings; they take breaks or reschedule if the tone is stale or fretful. Pushing through is neither wise nor productive. If the mind is clogged, it needs fresh thinking.

Alignment is Non-Contingent

What if everyone is not in a clear mind at the same time? Of course this will happen. But one person's clear mind is not contingent on someone else. When more people are clear, open, curious, and listen to learn, there is a gravitational pull in the direction of clarity.

There is no desire to enter into "I told you so," or "I never thought it would work." When roadblocks are encountered, a way is found around them. Decisions are made and changed or adjusted as needed.

Alignment Assumes Common Ground Exists

Perhaps you've heard this bit of advice, "Look for common ground where it exists." On its face, it may sound fine. But there is an underlying assumption that it may *not* exist. If that is the premise, there is no need to look because curiosity is limited by what is already known. There's no place to go.

Common ground may not be immediately apparent, but it will always become clear when minds are open and curious and people are listening to understand. If there isn't *enough* common ground, perhaps the specifications for decision making need to be revisited.

Alignment Must Be Tested

Sometimes it's so exhilarating when a decision is made, there is a tendency to tear out of the room and leap tall buildings. But, wait. The job is not done.

How do you test for alignment? You ask questions.

Questions to Test Alignment

Who else do we need to hear from?

You may need to hear from other experts, people who will be affected, and people who will need to implement. The same respect is afforded to the guests as to the members of the team.

Does everyone agree with the decision? Is it final or is there wiggle room?

There does not need to be agreement with every aspect of the approach. It is a priority that all members feel included and have an opportunity to contribute. There is plenty of room to disagree, test ideas, change or add assumptions, and revise specifications along the way. Alignment means you are not just willing to live with the decision, but will be an active supporter and fully engaged in its execution.

How will the decision be communicated? When and by whom?

Articulate what you plan to say and deliver. Discuss how you will teach others what they need to know. If the decision is final, be clear about it.

Is there a test period to see how the decision works?

Be leery about the plan for implementation, testing, and measurement. If there is a need for training, it needs to be clear who is accountable for it, who is responsible for the actual training, and how all those involved will be brought on board. The project may also be a development opportunity for someone, and that should also be discussed.

When will you reassess the plan and implementation? How will you know it is a success? How will you know when to pull the plug?

A plan of review is not only wise, it is essential, and it should include the possibility that the decision made may have a finite lifetime of utility.

There will be plenty of questions that need to be addressed, including these mentioned. However, when the proper dialogue has occurred to explore the purpose, need, possible approaches and who needs to be involved, the decision is often fairly swift.

Bottom Line

Aligned teams are thorough and operate from a mind-set of value for each other, respect, trust, listening for clarity, and rapport. Meetings tend to be smooth and efficient as well as effective. Members of the team find they are working diligently and yet enjoy the process and the people.

The state of mind *and* the outcome of alignment become the norm rather than a stroke of luck.

Reflective Questions

What resonates with you in this chapter?

What surprises you about this chapter?

What are you curious to learn more about?

Bonus Question

How aligned are the teams you lead or participate in? How could you contribute to increasing the likelihood of alignment?

My Insights

Products and Services

Products

Books:

We Declare: The Truth About War and Our Responsibility for Peace

He Called Me Lieutenant Angel: A Love Song From War

Power of a Clear Mind: The Direct Link Between Your Leadership State of Mind, The Decisions You Make, The Actions You Take, The Results You Get

Audio CDs:

Power of a Clear Mind: Keep Your Bearings in *Any* Circumstance

The 8 Essential Ingredients of Healing: From *Anything, Anywhere, Anytime*

Services

Executive Consulting & Coaching: Individual and Executive Teams

Transfer of Competency: Workshops for Consultants and Coaches

Speaker: Key-Note and Conference Speaker

Learn More

To order or to learn more about Penny's Products and Services, visit: www.powerofaclearmind.com. Penny may be contacted directly at: penny@powerofaclearmind.com

About the Author

Penny Rock is an International Executive Consultant and Coach, Inspirational Speaker, and Author. A recognized leader in the dynamics of healthy thinking, her "Power of a Clear Mind" principles and concepts have been integrated into the private and public sectors.

The foundation of her methodology is her belief in the unlimited potential for greatness that resides in each human being. *"Unleashing, and having faith in our innate wisdom mobilizes us to create a healthier home, business, and world community."*

Penny's twenty-two years of experience with CEO's and Senior Teams has taken her to the boardrooms of such companies as: British Telecom; Bell Atlantic; Blue Cross; Chase Bank; Discover Card; Hewlett Packard; International Truck and Engine; Cummins South Africa and Ghana, the Philadelphia Orchestra, and many others. BA and MBA degrees in Business, Leadership and Organization Development support her corporate background.

In addition, Penny's life experience as a Vietnam War Veteran and Breast Cancer Survivor enhances her ability to inspire others as a Keynote Speaker or Workshop Leader through her belief that *"Each person has the ability to transcend and benefit from any life experience."*

Penny was featured in the Academy Award nominated documentary film "A Healing." She is the inspiration for Normi Noel's play *"No Background Music"*, originally produced by Shakespeare & Company in August 2006. Adapted for BBC World Wide Radio, it premiered in September 2005, and won the Sony Gold Drama award 2006. Penny was portrayed by Sigourney Weaver.

Penny is the author of the books, *He Called Me Lieutenant Angel: A Love Song from War,* and *We Declare: The Truth About War and Our Responsibility for Peace.* She has recorded the audio CDs, *Power of a Clear Mind*, and *The 8 Essential Ingredients of Healing.* Penny is now completing her next book, *Power of a Clear Mind: Keep Your Bearings in ANY Circumstance.*

The Founder and President of the Executive Consulting & Coaching Company *Power of a Clear Mind,* Penny may be contacted at: penny@powerofaclearmind.com.